Justice for Women

The Cry to End the Pandemic of Discrimination, Intimidation, Misogyny, Abuse, and Violence against Women in Society and Religious Communities

ISBN: 9798856320694

"The story of women's struggle for equality belongs to no single feminist nor any one organisation but to the collective efforts of all who care about human rights."
Gloria Steinem

"But let justice roll on like a river, righteousness like a never-failing stream!" Amos 5:6

"Justice, in its broadest sense, is the concept that individuals are to be treated in a manner that is equitable and fair."
Margaret Moore

DEDICATION

I dedicate this book to you, my reader: to every man who has encountered at least one woman who impacted his life positively, and to every woman who has witnessed and or experienced inequity, injustice, humiliation and discrimination for being female. I dedicate this book to the game-changers: every President, Governor, Prime Minister, Secretary, Treasurer, Administrator, Executive member, Pastor, Reverend, Bishop, Vicar, Imam, Rabbi, Teacher, Manager, Director, Executive Producer, Artist, Nurse, Elder, Board Member, Church Member, Teacher, Educational and Academic Institution, Other Groups, Individuals, Enquiring Minds and Agents of Change to *End the Pandemic of Discrimination, Intimidation, Misogyny, Abuse and Violence against Women in Society and Religious Communities that women can have Value, Visibility, Voice and Vocational Equality.*

"When women are empowered, they immeasurably improve the lives of everyone around them—their families, their communities, and their countries. This is not just about women; we men need to recognise the part we play too. Real men treat women with dignity and give them the respect they deserve." Prince Harry, Duke of Sussex.

TABLE OF CONTENTS

FOREWORD

For centuries the cry for women to be treated respectfully, fairly, and equally has often gone unheard. *Justice for Women: The Cry to End the Pandemic of Discrimination, Intimidation, Misogyny, Abuse, and Violence against Women in Society and Religious Communities* challenges in a systematic, coherent, and respectful manner, the underlying beliefs, presuppositions, and attitudes about women that have been handed down over the centuries which distort, demean, demoralise, and discriminate against women; the very grounds upon which gender-based violence, crimes and discrimination against women are often predicated.

The author challenges the widely held interpretations of the controversial sayings in the Bible about women which seem to suggest that women were somehow created less than equal to men; (ontological inequality) and that their role in eating the proverbial "fruit" or bringing sin into the world, relegates women to a role of submission to men (functional or role and vocational inequality) in the home, religious communities, and society. Biblical stories about women still influence the way women see themselves and the way men see women. Many narratives about women in sacred texts have been and are still being used pejoratively, resulting in women being discriminated against. Therefore, the truth about women must be told; this book does just that. The author has applied the disciplines of exegesis and hermeneutics so that every reader can be empowered to refute the traditional arguments that have too long been tendered to substantiate discrimination against women in society.

Finally, a must-read book that is a balanced, well-researched, sensitive exploration of a topic that continues to cause pain and despair. Aptly described as a 'pandemic', discrimination against women is a feature of this era of supposed exponential change and progress and is sadly perpetuated by an institution based on love. I am encouraged because we are asked to objectively review the foundations of our belief systems, reflect on our stewardship, and join in the call for justice. Kudos to Dr Jeanville for this life-changing masterpiece. An indispensable teaching tool for men and women of faith and non-faith alike on gender inclusiveness.

You have made a great choice to have this book in your hand.

Lorraine Vernal, PhD
Jamaica Union Conference
Mandeville

"Empowering women isn't just the right thing to do – it's the smart thing to do. When women succeed, nations are more safe, more secure, and more prosperous". Barack Obama, 44th U.S. President.

KAREN HOLFORD

I never imagined I would be a leader.

Not me, a little girl who was so shy that I hid in cupboards at social events. When I was a teenager, I decided again that I wouldn't be a leader. I'd seen leaders, mostly men, and they were often loud, rough, powerful, and controlling, and I, most certainly, was none of those things. So, no, I wouldn't be a leader...And then I married my husband, Bernie Holford. And, within the first few months, he had taken me by the hand and gently started to nudge me out of the cupboard. Little by little he encouraged me onto the platform, to speak with him. At first, it was a few words, and then a story to illustrate the relationship seminars that we taught, and then I was writing scripts and we were presenting them as equals.

When Bernie was asked to work in Scotland as a church administrator. My safe little space fell apart again. There was no work for me in Scotland. I worked as a volunteer family therapist, here and there. Then I was a family therapy trainer, a publicist, and a writer. I was doing so many different things...I paused to reflect on what I loved to do the most. It was training people and creating resources...Two weeks later I received a call asking me to be the director of family ministries at the Trans European Division of Seventh-day Adventists (TED). 'What will that involve?' I asked. 'Training people and creating resources.' I smiled... God was trying to tell me something...

So, Bernie resigned from his job as the Conference President in Scotland to return to local church pastoring. 'You have followed me all your life, now it is my turn to follow you.' He set aside his leadership position, empowering me to lead at almost the highest level that a woman can lead in our church in Europe. I continue to work and grow there, thanks to the gentle guidance, empowerment and mentoring of wise, caring, and supportive men: my husband, Bernie, Drs Erich Baumgartner and Randy Siebold, who taught me leadership skills, and Dr Daniel Duda, the TED president, who continues to stretch, support, and empower me in ways that I never would have thought possible. Thanks to all of you for being men who are not afraid to lift women and empower them to fly.

I am so delighted to see that now my friend, Dr Jude Jeanville, has dedicated many years of study and work on the vital topic of breaking the bonds of oppression, correcting distorted beliefs, challenging stereotypes, and calling out the misuse of power, abuse, and fear that many of us have faced as women. I cannot thank him enough for writing this amazing book that explores so many aspects of deep-seated injustice. I hope and pray that what he has written will challenge hearts and minds and bring hope and healing to the lives of both women and men. May we work together in peace, respect and love to build a healthy, just, balanced, and loving society, where everyone can flourish and grow, and change the climate in our world for women and a better place for all.

May God bless you for your love, humility and courage.
Karen Holford
General Conference of Seventh-day Adventists
Trans-European Division

"I always did something I was a little not ready to do. I think that's how you grow. When there's that moment of 'Wow, I'm not really sure I can do this,' and you push through those moments, that's when you have a breakthrough." – Marissa Mayer

ACKNOWLEDGEMENTS

Gratitude to the University of the Southern Caribbean (USC) from where I conducted my research on gender inclusiveness, and to the Chairperson of the board of trustees of the USC, the President of the Caribbean Union Conference of Seventh-day Adventists, Dr Kern Tobias, and his predecessor, Dr Eugene Daniel for being part sponsors of my Doctor of Ministry degrees in Family Life and Preaching.

To the incumbent President of the University of the Southern Caribbean, Dr Colwick M. Wilson, and his predecessors, Dr Hilary Bowman, Dr Clinton Anthony Valley, Dr Trevor Gardner, Dr Shirley Ann Mc Garrell, Dr Sylvan Lashley, Dr Leslie T. Ferdinand, Dr Vernon Andrews, Dr John Ambrose and my personal friends and mentors, Drs Roy and Shirley Ann Mc Garrell, whose invaluable contribution to my academic, professional and personal development would always be remembered. To Pastor Anthony Hall, President of East Caribbean Conference and Pastor Leslie Moses, President of the South Caribbean Conference, Pastors and Bible Workers for participating in the research survey, and to Pastor Henry Snagg, former Pastor of the University Church, and Pastor Terry Alva John, Vice President of Spiritual Affairs who graciously facilitated my practicum at the university.

I commenced my doctoral studies in Family Life at Andrews University, Berrien Springs, Michigan, after two years of sound lecturing, I enrolled at North Park University, Chicago, USA and graduated with the Doctor of Ministry in Preaching. I had the privilege of studying with clergy and lay people from many denominations on the Campus of Mc Cormick Theological Seminary, Chicago, for 3 years, just two blocks away from the private residence of Mr. and Mrs. Barack Obama (Former President of the United States of America and the First Lady).

Special thanks to my Advisor, Dr Carol Norén; the members of my Parish Project Group (PPG): Pastor Ronald Daniel (Chair), Dr Sandra Reid, Phil Williams, Sherwayne Cort, Rachel Sealy, and Nora Lopez, whose objective and thought-provoking insights, deliberations, and gracious feedback helped improve my homiletical and exegetical skills. They untiringly and selflessly invested in my professional development.

Deep appreciation to my parents, Paulina and Joseph Jeanville; my seven aunties and brother-in-law, Paul Phillip and sister Mary Jasmine Phillip, all now deceased. Ann Baker-Jeanville, Annette Baker-Richardson, Merle Mollenthiel, Rhea Diaz, Schereen Samaroosingh, Sheena Diaz, my siblings—Jesse Jeanville, Mary Phillip, Magdalene Tobias, Martha Valley, Miriam Legall, Joel Jueanville, John Jueanville and their spouses; my three children, Joel Jueanville, Melanie-Marie Holder and Melinda Boachie, and their mother, Marva Golden and sons-in-law, Kobi and Nathan. To my grandchildren, Adeya-May Haywood, Essie-Quin Boachie, and Naïma Rae Holder, and all my nieces, nephews, and cousins. Also, my dear Sandra Herbert, Domonique, Patrice and Miles Herbert, Maizie and Victor Fletcher, Cris, Sheyan and Jehan Walter, Sheila Rachael Pierre (nee Deterville), Simone Augustus, Keith Smith, Mike and Carol Coleman and Maureen and Ignaz Kerr, whose friendship and support I drew on. A special thank you to Pastor Lester Parkinson, Rear Admiral Barry C. Black (Retired Chief of Chaplains of the United States Navy) and Dr Wintley Phipps, founder of the U.S Dream Academy. To former presidents, Pastors Ronald Surridge, Egerton Francis, Mike Stickland (all deceased), Pastor Freddie Russell and Pastor Humphrey Walters, Dr Sam Davis, Dr Richard de Lisser, Dr Emmanuel Osei, and the incumbent president of the South England Conference, Dr Kirk Thomas.

Dr Abraham Jules, President of Northeastern Conference, Dr Blassious Ruguri, President, Eastern Africa Division and Dr Michael Campbell, North American Division.

Tottenham Lighthouse, Wood Green, and Barnet SDA churches, my Ministerial Colleagues in Area 6A, London; Pastors Carl

Thorpe, David Burnett, Valentine Roach and Pastor Everett Brown, President of Jamaica Union Conference; Pastor Levi Johnson, Vice President; Dr Dudley Hosin, Director of Health and Publishing Ministries; Dr Stephen Agilinko, Minister of the West Green Baptist Church and George Myristis, Managing Director, 257 West Green Road, Tottenham, London.

To multiple time author, Mrs Sharon Platt-McDonald whose professional experience in writing and editing was invaluable, and her husband Denzle for his personal encouragement.

My penultimate thanks go to my 5AM prayer group.

Finally, my deepest gratitude is reserved for God, my "Ezer" (Hebrew for "Helper").

WOMEN OF INFLUENCE IN OUR LIFETIME

Women, who, despite the odds, have said, "Yes we can",[1] and have left an indelible mark on theircommunity and the world. The story of many a woman is reflected in the narratives of at least one of these women listed opposite: (By no means an exhaustive list)

---

[1] Barak Obama's speech to supporters after losing the New Hampshire's Democratic primary to Hilary Clinton on 8 January 2008. NPR. https://www.npr.org/2008/11/05/96624326/transcript-of-barack-obamas-victory-speech. (Accessed June 7, 2023).

Her Late Majesty Queen
Elizabeth The Second

Her Excellency the Most
Honourable Lady Allen

Heather-Dawn Small

Audrey Andersson

Karen Holford

Sharon Platt-
McDonald

Judy Clements OBE

Lorraine Vernal

Mother Teresa

Kamala Harris

Brenda Walsh

Jacqueline Otopka

Beulah Plunkett

Anne-May Müller

Mia Mottley

Michelle Obama

Princess Diana

Emma Watson

Margaret Thatcher

Hillary Clinton

Petra Tunheim

Elisabeth Sangüesa

Ai Araki

Elizabeth Sterndale

Consolacion Tauro

Phyllis Ware-Lee

Oprah Winfrey

Whitney Houston

Serena Williams

Gillian Joseph

Theresa May MP

Diane Abbott MP

Andrea Luxton

Linda Tobias

Sandra E. Roberts

Lottie Blake

Karen Flowers

Joy Fehr

Joan de Lisser

Ginger Ketting-Weller

Wilma Glodean Rudolph

Lisa Smith-Reid

Rowena Davis

Heather Haworth

Rosa Taylor Banks

Prudence Pollard

Susan B. Anthony

Vanita Sauder

Siriporn Tanitpoonwinai

Anna Knight

Estée Lauder

Rosa Parks

Councillor Gina Adamou

Amelia Earhart

Jane Goodhall

Ella Louise Smith
Simmons

Olga Murga

Marcia Brandon

Heather Knight

Margaret Ramsaran

Hanane Lyettefti

Ruth Handler

Gloria Steinem

Alma Perry

Mary McFarlane

Cynthia Southcott

Florence
Nightingale

Eleanor Roosevelt

Donnett Blake

Councillor Peray Ahmet

Councillor Michelle
Simmons-Safo

Councillor Barbara Blake

Eve Ricketts

Diana McIntyre-Pike

Helen Keller

Edith Samambwa

Margaret Hamilton

Emmeline Panklhurst

Denneese Thorpe

Michelle Moore

Janice Mingo

Frida Kahlo

Nancy Pelosi

Mary Kay Ash

Judith Azare

Marie Curie

Victoria Pritchard

Sally Ride

Trudean Scott-Elliott

Madeleine Albright

Barbara Jordan

Anita Scott

Condoleezza Rice

Junko Tabei

Harriet Tubman

Indira Gandhi

Irena Sendler

Clara Barton

Laura Osei

Gina Abbequaye

Ann Swaby

Althea Gibson

Graca Machel

Christine Kangaloo

Valentina Tereshkova

Sandra Day O'Connor

Maya Angelou

Mae Jemison

Benazir Bhutto

Priscilla Provost

Marilyn Monroe

Aretha Franklin

Olive Hemmings

Prudence Pollard

Kamla Persad-Bissessar

Patricia Manning

Eugenia Charles

Hyveth Williams

Sandra Reid

Shirley Mc Garrell

Merna Riley-
desVignes

Leola Robert-Withers

Mary Ferdinand

Candy Layson

Michelle Vernon

Audrey Soyam

Maxine Donovan

Petra Pierre-Robertson

Edwina Mc Farquhar-
Wilson

Mary Jasmine Phillip

Mavis Haywood

Sophie Charles

Claudette James

Maslin Holness

Marion Wadibia

Vilma Virginia
Redican-Elliott

Beverley King

Angela Merkel

Sheikh Hassina Wajed

Nicola Sturgeon

Saara Kuugongelwa

Bidhya Devi Bhandari

Ava Walters

Venus Williams

Rose Hudson-Wilkin

Mette Frederiksen

Kersti Kaljulaid

Tsai Ing-Wen

Ana Brnabić

Yvonne Noel-Bruno

Halimah Jakob

Jacinda Ardern

Jenifer Sweeney

Katrin Jakobsdo'ttir

Sahle Work-Zewde

Salome Zourabichvili

Jacquelyn Johnson

Paula-Mae Weekes

Giorgia Meloni

Catherine Boldeau

Sanna Marin

Zuzana Caputova

Maia Sandu

Katerina Sakellaropoulou

Ingrida Simonyte

Rose Christiane Raponda

Saojiah Vernon

Decila Agnes Roberts

Rosemary Lethbridge

Nerine Barrett

Ssashoi Ellis Tate

Amanda Gorman

Odele Prince

Desaline Joseph-Simon

Carol Thomas

Tina Brooks

Abena Osei-Poku

Ethel Cofie

Amina Adamu Augie

Josephine Joseph (nee Mattie)

Gina Miller

Njoki Ndungu

Fernanda Montenegro

Ivete Sangalo

Ségolène Royal

Sophia Peart

Val Bernard – Allan

Fedilia Maxwin (Edna)

Wanda Chesney

Rachel Sealey

Serene Allen

Adele Laurie Blue
Adkins MBE

Winnie Mandela

Swati Dlamini Mandela

DeeAnn Bragaw

Fiona Pacquette

Mary Seacole

Portia Simpson Miller

Anita Erskine

Finn F. Eckhoff

Kemi Badenoch

Mary Barrett

Mary Kapon

Pat Modeste

Mikella Semper

Elizabeth Semper

Thembie Mapingire

Flora Plummer

Kim Malgas

Lady Liz Green

Mariam Hassam

Kenisha Jackson

Angela Jackson OBE

Agartha Baldwin

Greta Tintin Eleonora

Ernman Thunberg

Justice for Women: The Cry to End the Pandemic of Discrimination, Intimidation, Misogyny, Abuse and Violence against Women in Society and Religious Communities.

INTRODUCTION

The book you are holding in your hands is a game-changer for our world, particularly for women and girls. A book that every man needs to read. The call for women to be respected and treated equally as fellow human beings has reverberated across all levels of society for a long time. Every day, the media report on gender-based crimes against women and girls, such as sexual harassment, sexist behaviour, stalking, rape, domestic violence, emotional abuse, silent bullying, financial abuse, religious abuse, human trafficking, disparaging abuse on social media, and other forms of discrimination in the home, workplace, and society. These are just some of the hazards that come with living in a woman's skin. Certainly, this cannot be considered justice.

Violence Against Women and Girls (VAWG) is a term adopted from the United Nations 1993 declaration that includes "Any act of gender-based violence that results in, or is likely to result in, physical, sexual or psychological harm or suffering to women, including threats of such acts, coercion or arbitrary deprivation of liberty, whether occurring in public or in private life."[2]

"1 in 7 women and 1 in 25 men have been injured by an intimate partner.

1 in 10 women have been raped by an intimate partner. Data is unavailable on male victims. 1 in 4 women and 1 in 7 men have been victims of severe physical violence (e.g., beating, burning, strangling) by an intimate partner in their lifetime.

---

[2] World Health Organization. https://www.who.int/ health-topics/violence-against-women. (Accessed June 7, 2023).

1 in 7 women and 1 in 18 men have been stalked by an intimate partner during their lifetime to the point in which they felt very fearful or believed that they or someone close to them would be harmed or killed."[3]

"In the United Kingdom between the year ending March 2018 and March 2020, 76% of victims of domestic homicide were female, and 14% of victims of non-domestic homicide were female."[4]

Isn't society tired of hearing about women and girls who are the primary targets of crime, violence, abuse, and discrimination? "If you talk to five women, three of them would likely share horror stories of living in a female's body. Women face risks from birth and throughout their lifetime from molestation, harassment, intimidation, bullying, and physical and emotional abuse, particularly from males. Being a woman is far from easy."[5] Has our society become desensitised to the abuse of women and girls? Has our lack of consistent cohesive effort to end gender discrimination normalized this type of behaviour?

Alongside the nauseating abuse of women and girls, millions of women are discriminated against; they are underpaid for the same jobs as their male counterparts; and they are not given equal opportunities for upward mobility, simply because of their gender.

Up until the 20th century, women did not have a vote or voice in politics. Many of the laws women are subject to were made by men. The Baroness Kennedy of The Shaws KC, in the United Kingdom, said in an International Women's Day speech: "You don't have to believe in patriarchy to realise that the law was made by men and is dominated by men and that the same goes for

---

[3] National Intimate Partner and Sexual Violence Survey: 2010 Summary Report. https://www.cdc.gov/violenceprevention/pdf/nisvs_report2010-a.pdf. (Accessed June 7, 2023).
[4] Office of National Statistics. www.ons.gov.uk/peoplepopulationandcommunity/crimeandjustice/articles/domesticabusevictimcharacteristicsenglandandwales. Year ending March 2021. (Accessed June 7, 2023).
[5] Sabena Christian, telephone interview, June 6, 2023.

parliament. This means that in all the making of the law, women are largely absent. It is not surprising that the law doesn't work for women."[6]

Gender discrimination is a pandemic because every woman and girl at some point in their lifetime would experience crime, discrimination, or abuse because of their gender.

Institutions and large corporations are built on misogynistic policies that discriminate against women. In the United Kingdom, large corporations like the British Broadcasting Corporation (BBC) were sued for misogynistic policies. "An employment tribunal unanimously concluded that the BBC had failed to provide convincing evidence that the pay gap was for reasons other than gender discrimination, although the BBC continues to dispute this."[7]

The former chief crown prosecutor for the Northwest, Nazir Afzal, author of an independent review, said that the London Fire Brigade (LFB) is "institutionally misogynist and racist" with a "toxic culture that allows bullying and abuse". Afzal said that they "found dangerous levels of ingrained prejudice against women, and the barriers faced by people of colour spoke for themselves."[8]

In the United States of America, a lawsuit filed in a San Francisco court says Google, "discriminated against female staff with lower pay, more limited promotion, and fewer advancement opportunities compared to men with comparable qualifications."[9] Similar scenarios can be duplicated all around the world.

---

[6] The Guardian Newspaper of the Year. https://www. theguardian.com/global-development/2014/sep/29/women-better-off-far-from-equal-men. (Accessed June 7, 2023).

[7] https://www.theguardian.com/media/2020/jan/10/samira-ahmedwins-equal-pay-claim-against-bbc. (Accessed December 2, 2021).

[8] Evening Standard. https://www.standard.co.uk/ news/london/london-fire-brigade-misogyny-racism-grenfell-independent-review-b1042777.html. (Accessed June 7, 2023).

[9] https://www.nytimes.com/2022/06/12/business/google-discrimination-settlement-women.html#. (Accessed June 2023).

The Church, the Church Fathers, and Women

Biases against women are deep-seated. These biases can be traced to religious and philosophical teachings, cultural norms and practices, and institutional policies that have been formulated and enforced on the damaging notion of gender inequality.

The debate on the role of women in the home, church, and society, though extremely divisive, is far too significant to be swept under the rug. In Christianity, other faith groups, and society, there is a split over the nature and role of women. I respectfully recognise the sensitivities surrounding the subject of the role of women in different cultures worldwide and therefore approach this topic with great care, respect, and integrity, however, we must have a sense of appreciation as to how we got where we are today if we are to effectively change the narrative of women and girls in our society.

How did we get here? The Christian worldview teaches that God made male and female in his image and likeness, meaning that both males and females possess and reflect God's attributes of love, unity, and equality. The same characteristics that exist in the Godhead are characteristic of males and females alike. These characteristics of love, unity, and equality are also fundamental to harmonious interpersonal relationships between males and females. Therefore, the Genesis account teaches the equality of males and females as an essential characteristic of God, not optional but constitutional.

However, history records the warped views of some theologians and Church Fathers, (from about 160 AD) which today would be unacceptable and branded misogynistic. Rather disturbing and crude presuppositions about women have influenced the Church's theology on an ontological difference between males and females, either at creation or thereafter, which has given rise to the silencing and subordination of women and a justification for male headship and male privilege, the basis of abuse and discrimination against women.

I invite you to examine three ill-founded presuppositions at the heart of misogyny, patriarchy, gender privilege, and discrimination of women which this book adequately addresses:

1. The superiority of males over females. The creation account of a man being created first, and a woman second as a helpmeet, gives males an ontological advantage over females. Intrinsic or ontological inequality (or inequality by nature).

2. That the woman's seduction by the serpent, and the ensuing consequence for her role in the entrance of sin into the world, relegated all women to a position of perpetual subordination, submission, and silence (functional inequality).

3. That the Apostle Paul's injunctions for women to keep silent in the churches and not teach or exercise authority are universal commands to all women, which limit women vocationally.

Church Fathers.

According to Scholer "Ancient Judaism literature reflects a negative view toward women. He writes that Josephus, a Jewish historian, points to the Law that declares "women to be inferior in all matters... should be submissive"; Philo, a Jewish philosopher, "argues that women ought to stay at home, desiring a life of seclusion"; Sirach, an Apocrypha book, states, "better is the wickedness of a man than a woman who does good; it is a woman who brings shame and disgrace." (Sir. 42:14 NRSV)[10]

Saint Augustine believed that women were only created for reproduction and were deficient in the image of God as was man. He said, "It is still Eve the temptress that we must beware of in any woman."[11]

Saint Thomas Aquinas, once said," Woman is defective and

---

[10] David M. Scholer, "Women," in Dictionary of Jesus and the Gospels, ed. Joel B. Green, Scot McKnight, and I. Howard Marshall (Downers Grove, IL: InterVarsity, 1992), p. 886.
[11] https://www.jstor.org/stable/41178077. (Accessed August 2022).

misbegotten."[12]

Tertullian said of women, "You are the devil's gate. God's sentence hangs still over all your sex, and His punishment weighs over you. You are the devil's gateway; you are she who first violated the forbidden tree and broke the law of God. It was you who coaxed your way around him whom the devil did not have the force to attack. With what ease you shattered that image of God: man! Because of the death you merited, the son of God had to die."[13]

"Aristotle (383-322 BCE) was one of a trio of philosophers and teachers in Ancient Greece (along with Socrates and Plato) who helped shape the foundations of Western thought. He arrived in Athens from Northern Greece as an orphaned teenager to study under Plato who himself had earlier studied under Socrates. Later as a teacher on his own, Aristotle helped tutor the young Alexander the Great. Aristotle maintained that it is precisely because the male is by nature superior and the female inferior that the one rules and the other is ruled."[14]

David Balch "indicates a virtually universal perception that women were to be ruled by men, usually with the assumption that they were inferior to men. In context, the teaching "wives submit to your husbands" will sound quite normal to the woman being addressed. It was what their pagan society had always taught."[15] Repugnant, to say the least.

"The Theologians from Augustine to Aquinas to Luther, Wesley, and Bath were men. Women were excluded from this Elite Club. "No Daughters of Eve Allowed" would have been a fitting sign on

---

[12] F. Forrester Church. The Harvard Theological Review, Vol. 68, No. 2 (Apr.1975), p. 1 (Cambridge University Press). https://www.jstor.org/stable/1509087. (Accessed June 8, 2023).
[13] Ibid.
[14] Aristotle, *Politics* (350 BCE), Book One, Parts V-VII, https://housedivided.dickinson.edu/sites/teagle/texts/ aristotle-politics-350-bce/. (Accessed June 2023).

[15] Pierce and Groothius, p, 227.

the clubhouse door...That she was more easily deceived than the man and would have been a menacing presence in the ivory towers of theological discussions and decision making."[16]

Unfortunately, the warped views of some theologians, Church Fathers, and philosophers have influenced the teachings of the Christian Church on women, and the widespread influence of Christianity has helped to give legitimacy to patriarchy and misogyny, globally. These notions contribute to the way women are seen and treated as inferior or less than, and not equal to men.

Unlike the views of some Church Fathers, females possess intellectual capacity no less than men, "male and female created he them; in the image of God, created he them". (Genesis 1:27) Therefore, ontologically speaking, females were created in the image of God where there is no trace of inferiority.

Beyond any doubt, our generation has inherited these misbegotten notions about women which are deeply engrained into the psyche of many and have even been institutionalised in segments of society.

Despite such warped views by some Church Fathers, theologians, and historians who caricatured women in such poor light, "There are women who gave their lives to monastic teachings and living: Marcella of Rome, Monica the mother of Saint Augustine and Susanna Wesley, mother of John and Charles Wesley, Catherine of Siena, Gertrude of Hefla and Hildegard of Bingen. Some of these women were known as mystics, many throughout medieval times, who challenged the established church to return to holiness."[17] They received theological insight through visions and revelations, but never did they reach the statue of great theologians such as Anselm and Thomas Aquinas or Peter Lombard."[18]

Whether one is a person of faith or not, the Christian worldview

---

[16] Ibid., p. 26.
[17] Ibid., p. 27.
[18] Ibid.

has and continues to play a prominent role in shaping the values of Western civilization through biblical stories and characters, many of which have become part of the fabric of our lives. Biblical stories or narratives continue to influence our thinking today, particularly, stories about women. Women's stories are incredibly popular. On the one hand, we have characters or women who are renowned and emulated, and on the other, we have those who are cited in notoriously pejorative ways.

For example, do you know of any female by the name of Jezebel? I don't. I believe this could be so because the name is associated with disparaging characteristics of a woman in the Bible; Jezebel is seen as an unstoppably evil, wicked woman. (1 King 18-21, 21:25, 2 Kings 9:37, Revelation 2:20) No mother has chosen that name for their daughter as a first or second choice. On the other hand, I am sure you know or have heard about a female by the name of Eve, the first woman in the creation account, Deborah, the first female judge and prophet, or Esther the queen, because of the association of these names in biblical stories. Sadly, despite these heroic stories of feminine intuition and vocational leadership in the scriptures in what was considered a patriarchal society, certain passages of the scriptures have been ill-used deploying the Proof Text method to formulate and perpetuate a theology about women that limits, distorts, demeans, demoralizes, and discriminates against women, contributing to the pandemic of discrimination against women and what I call, gendered spaces.

Churches

In Protestantism and Roman Catholicism (Christianity), there is a failure to interpret a few passages of the scriptures, accurately, "Rightly dividing the word of truth" or (to do exegesis and hermeneutics effectively) consequently, the Churches have failed to tell the stories about women who in patriarchal times, equally occupied positions of authority and influence; women who were not the exceptions, but the rule.

Within Protestantism, some denominations like the Methodist Church and the Evangelical Covenant Church practice equality for women, for the best part of fifty years, they have given women equal status in the church. The Anglican Church has taken a clear stand on ordaining women Bishops, kudos to them. They have intentionally shaped and applied policies for the full participation of women at all levels in their organisations based on the correct interpretation of the scriptures.

In the Roman Catholic Church, there is no question concerning a woman's ontology (nature). In his encyclical *Familiaris Consortio: The Role of the Christian Family in the Modern World*, Pope John Paul II explains, "In creating the human race "male and female," **God gives man and woman an equal personal dignity . . . God then manifests the dignity of women in the highest form possible, by assuming human flesh from the Virgin Mary, whom the Church honours as the 'Mother of God'**.

I commend the Roman Catholic Church for such a profound statement on ontological equality and the dignity of women. When it comes to role equality, however, a woman will not be considered part of the established clergy or liturgy. In 1993, a group of women and men who care deeply about the Roman Catholic Church began what is known as "Catholic Women's Ordination" said, "We want to be a part of building a church community that truly lives the justice demanded by Jesus; a justice which demands that women be equal with men".[19] Other major world religions practice the same dichotomy of claiming gender or ontological equality while practicing functional inequality.

The Seventh-day Adventist Church has a powerful statement on gender equality which reads "Seventh-day Adventists believe that all people, male and female, are created equal, in the image of a loving God. We believe that both men and women are called to fill a significant role in accomplishing the primary mission of the Adventist Church: working together for the benefit of

---

[19] **Catholic Women's Ordination: Challenging Institutional Misogyny in the Roman Catholic Church.** https://www.catholic-womens-ordination.org.uk. (Accessed June 8, 2023).

humanity. Yet we are painfully aware that throughout the world, in developing and developed nations, adverse societal conditions often inhibit women from fulfilling their God-given potential."

Although the Seventh-day Adventist Church has a theologically sound statement on ontological and functional equality for women, the church fails to execute functional equality in its policies and practice as acknowledged, "We are painfully aware that throughout the world, in developing and developed nations, adverse societal conditions often inhibit women from fulfilling their God-given potential".[20] It appears that the SDA Church does not have a biblical issue with the equality of women but acknowledges a sociological one.

Is it really "adverse societal conditions" or has the Church failed to establish a theology of women that supports women to equally fulfil their God given potential as do men?

Those who support ontological equality for women in the church are sometimes referred to as Egalitarians, they accept ontological (nature) equality of both males and females at creation and after "The fall", a term used for the entrance of sin. However, those who support ontological equality at creation but resist the idea of functional equality for women in the church, home, and society are referred to as Complementarians.

Feminists like Elizabeth Cady Stanton have taken issue with the Church because of its misinterpretation of the Bible, which has laid the foundation for male privilege and discrimination of women for millennia. "The Bible teaches that woman brought sin and death into the world that she precipitated the fall of the race, that she was arraigned before the judgment seat of Heaven, tried, condemned, and sentenced. Marriage for her was to be a condition of bondage, maternity a period of suffering and anguish, and in silence and subjection, she was to play the role of a dependent on man's bounty for all her material wants, and for all the information she might desire on the vital questions of the

[20] https://www.healthministries.com/all%20resources/womens-issues/?searchsite=gc.adventist.org. (Accessed August 6, 2023).

hour, she was commanded to ask her husband at home. Here is the Bible's position of women briefly summed up...The canon law, church ordinances, and scriptures are homogeneous, and all reflect the same spirit and sentiments...

These familiar texts are quoted by clergymen in their pulpits, by statesmen in the halls of legislation, by lawyers in the courts, and are echoed by the press of all civilized nations and accepted by the woman herself as "The Word of God." So perverted is the religious element in her nature, that with faith and works she is the chief support of the church and clergy; the very powers that make her emancipation impossible...When, in the early part of the Nineteenth Century, women began to protest against their civil and political degradation, they were referred to the Bible for an answer. When they protested against their unequal position in the church, they were referred to the Bible for an answer."[21]

In religious settings, female leaders are forced to find strategies to cope with the level of toxicity dished out at them. Not only do women face expected biases from men but they also must deal with women-to-women bias which is extremely caustic and toxic. I have heard extremely strong, reprehensible, and castigating comments by women about women ministers. Female ministers particularly face harassment, intimidation, bullying, misogyny, discrimination, rejection, contempt, isolation, abuse, prejudice, and hostility by fellow women and by males. Living in a woman's body can be hazardous for her health because of mental and physical stress, burnout, and sickness. The Church must call out the sin of misogyny and gender bias.

Whilst many positive things can be said about the Church and religious communities, some aspects require revisiting to avoid making the mistakes of the past. History documents the abuse of institutions and governments that embraced the Church's interpretation of the scriptures for their ends. The Church, for

---

[21] Elizabeth Cady Stanton. The Woman's Bible. https://www.sacred-texts.com/wmn/wb/wb02.htm. (Accessed June 8, 2023).

centuries, used the Bible to justify and condone slavery. Also, recently, the Irish government apologised for the Church's role and theology in creating a culture of abuse. The Church's theology led to thousands of young mothers who became pregnant out of wedlock, being ostracised, stigmatised, victimised, and sexually abused.[22] Inside and outside of the church, we see inequality's repercussions on broader society.

"The same discriminatory thinking lies behind the continuing gender gap in pay and why there are still so few women in office in the West. The root of this prejudice lies deep in our histories, but its impact is felt every day. It is not women and girls alone who suffer. It damages all of us. The evidence shows that investing in women and girls delivers major benefits for society."—*Jimmy Carter, 39th U.S. President.*

Historically, arguments for gender differences have cost women dearly. Women were assigned to roles and duties regarding the home and family while men were seen as the providers whose jobs were outside of the home. This motif still is prevalent today as some men do not think it is their responsibility to help keep the home, even in the face of women working just as men, outside of the home. Patriarchists (men who believe that they have more power than women) were successful in using the argument of a woman's unique reproductive capabilities (femininity linked to childbearing) as a reason for women not to pursue roles that were seen as masculine. This, of course, gave rise to the popular motif that a woman's place is in the home. It was only in the 19th century that the suffrage movement advocated for a woman's participation in public life and women were afforded a greater say. I am speaking about justice for women, surely this does not sound like justice.

No human being should be denied an equal opportunity because of their gender, ethnicity, religion, or disability. The

---

[22] https://www.ncronline.org/news/accountability/northern-irish-child-abuse-victims-get- government-apology. (Accessed August 23, 2022).

rights that belong to one belong to all. The Bible or other religious texts should not be used to exclude or discriminate against women, any person or group. The unalienable rights of every human being must be protected.

The American Declaration of Independence states "That all humankind are created equal, that they are endowed by their Creator with certain unalienable Rights, that among these are Life, Liberty, and the pursuit of Happiness", echoing John Locke's phrase "life, liberty, and property"[23]. (See the British equivalent, in the Equality Act, 2010).

According to definitions of justice Oxford Dictionary says Justice is: "1. *Administration of law or equity. 2. Maintenance of what is just or right by the exercise of authority or power; assignment of deserved reward or punishment; giving of due deserts.* Thesaurus: *corrective justice, distributive justice, indifferent justice, poetic justice, poetical justice, restorative justice, rough justice, social justice,* etc.: see the first element."[24]

"Modern frameworks include concepts such as distributive justice, egalitarianism, retributive justice, and restorative justice. Distributive justice considers what is fair based on what goods are to be distributed, between whom they are to be distributed, and what is the *proper* distribution. Egalitarians suggest justice can only exist within the coordinates of equality. Theories of retributive justice say justice is served by punishing wrongdoers, whereas restorative justice (also sometimes called "reparative justice") is an approach to justice that focuses on the needs of victims and offenders."[25]

---

[23] United States Declaration of Independence.
https://en.wikipedia.org/wiki/United_States_Declaration_of_Independence
. (2022, October 13).
[24] In *Wikipedia*. Oxford English Dictionary. https://www.oed.com/. view dictionary entry/Entry/102198.
[25] Justice. (2023, June 5). In *Wikipedia*.
https://en.wikipedia.org/wiki/Justice.

As a former Justice of the Peace, I took the judicial oath which said... "I will do right to all manner of people after the laws and usages of this realm, without fear or favour, affection or ill will." Justice then is doing right, and right is not left to a figment of the imagination or situational ethics but enshrined in the laws of God and the laws of the land. There are many philosophical, moral, and ethical considerations when speaking about justice. I believe, however, that justice is much more than a human or sociological construct, true justice emanates from divine justice. In the words of Margaret Moore, **Justice**, in its broadest sense, is the concept that individuals are to be treated in a manner that is equitable and fair."[26]

How females are seen and treated affects not only women but also every family, educational institution, business, church, religious organization, and society. "Women are immensely more than homemakers, spouses, and mothers: a fusion of attractive physiology and warm emotional connectivity. The rich attributes and diverse skills of the female species provide much to celebrate. However, this reality is often overlooked when women are viewed through the myopic lens of societal limitations."[27] This book seeks to rectify the distorted notions and beliefs about women, it seeks to rediscover the Value, Voice, Visibility, and Vocational equality that women, made in the image of God were designed to have.

Biography

I grew up in a patriarchal family, meaning, a family heavily influenced by the motif of male headship. I benefitted from the strong values of living in a religious home where my dad would frequently lay claim to being the "Head of the home" and would often cite the Bible to justify this position. Like many women of their generation, my mother knew that even if my father claimed to be the head, she was the neck! (Smile.) With what I call feminine intuition and wisdom; she would often use her neck to

---

[26] Ibid.

[27] Sharon Platt-McDonald, telephone interview, Watford, England. (June 2022).

turn the "head" in the needed direction. This context and the wider culture of the society in which I grew up, where there were clearly defined roles for women and entitlement for men developed in me a quest for the truth about the nature and role of women. After some thirty-five-plus years in academia, I've found the answers to the menacing arguments about women's nature, roles, and limitations in society.

Methodology

For my doctoral research, I developed a methodology that refutes the arguments often used to support the ontological and or functional inequality of women. I harmonised St. Paul's controversial sayings about women often cited as the grounds for a less than equal place for women, with the rest of the scriptures. A sample audience of participants from various countries agreed to be surveyed as part of the study. They were given a pre-survey on their perception of women's roles and then presented with narratives about women from the Bible. After examining those narratives, the same sample group was given a post-survey. The results confirmed that paying attention to women's narratives or stories in the Bible positively affirmed the perceptions of women's Value, Voice, and Vocational aptitude. ©

Chapter Summaries

The six succeeding chapters are dedicated to getting to the genesis of discrimination against women and restoring the elevated perspective God had in view when he created and redeemed women, made in their (Godhead) image and likeness. **It is hoped that the exegetical and hermeneutical insights about narratives of women from the Bible would serve as a methodology to re-examine the presuppositions upon which the foundation for the inequality of women in our society is predicated. Discovering the truth about women in the Bible is a catalyst to effectuate a change in the way women are seen and treated globally.** The Bible has been seen as the authoritative word of God for thousands of years and still is, unfortunately, its widespread influence has been accompanied by a misinterpretation of the nature and roles of women upon which the discrimination of women is often substantiated. This book redresses this misreckoning while preserving the harmony, synchronicity, and authenticity of the Bible.

Chapter 1. The Genesis of Gender: Created Equal crucially explores the basis for ontological equality – the equality of men and women at creation. The book of Genesis adequately treats the issues of human sexuality, gender, and more specifically, the ontology of women. When God said, "Let us make man in our image and likeness", they meant just that: that males and females would possess and reflect their attributes of love, unity, and equality. The same unity and equality that exists in the godhead is the very basis for harmonious interpersonal relationships between males and females. Therefore, Genesis teaches the equality of males and females as an essential characteristic of God.

"When God decided to assuage the loneliness of Adam by creating for him a "helpmeet" God did not give Adam someone inferior to him to help him out. This line of reasoning is not supported in the text, rather; God gave someone equal to Adam as the solution to his loneliness". **The Hebrew word "Ezer", translated as "Helpmeet" or "Helper" from the Hebrew expression "Ezer kenegdo" means "one who is the same as the other and who surrounds, protects, aids, helps, supports."**[28]

The woman, the "helpmeet" was made in the image of God (the equality between Father, Son, and Holy Spirit which I refer to as ontological equality) 1 John 5:7. In Genesis 2:23, Adam's words, "This is now bone of my bones and flesh of my flesh", is an affirmation of equality.[29] Therefore, in an unambiguous way, the Genesis account refutes the notion that women were created inferior to men, an argument used by Complementarians to

---

[28] https://godswordtowomen.org/help.htm. (Accessed March 12, 2017).
[29] Pierce, Ronald W. Groothuis, Rebecca Merrill Fee, Gordon D. Discovering Biblical Equality: Complementarity Without Hierarchy (Downers Grove, IL, InterVarsity Press, 2005), p. 86.

substantiate the limitation of women. According to Wikipedia, "Complementarianism is a theological view in Christianity, Judaism, and Islam, that men and women have different but *complementary* roles and responsibilities in marriage, family life and religious leadership."[30]

In the beginning, God created males and females in their image and likeness, both possessing the attributes of the Godhead, love, oneness, and equality; Eve being created from the side of Adam did not make her in any way inferior to him. This chapter also confirms that the first woman was given equal authority in the assignment, **to have dominion.** "And God said; let us make man in our image, after our likeness: **and let them have dominion** over the fish of the sea, and over the fowl of the air, and over the cattle, and over all the earth, and over every creeping thing that creepeth upon the earth." Genesis 1:26. **To have "dominion over the earth" is to have authority. Co-dominion was assigned to both man and woman, and over the earth, not dominion over one another, or domination of one another. God gave woman dominion or authority just as was man from the very beginning.**

This chapter refutes the notion held by some Church Fathers, philosophers, and theologians, that women were somehow created inferior to men, (ontological inequality and was not given a role of authority, (functional inequality) often defended on the woman's role in the entrance of sin in the world.

Chapter 2. Called and Gifted: Women in the Old Testament captures a theology of women who were endowed by God with gifts and abilities that made room for their various assignments, including leadership. Even against the backdrop of what was considered a patriarchal society where women and children were often taken as property during war, (Jeremiah 38:23) inspiration did not fail to record the narratives of women in God-given positions of power and influence. Deborah's narrative as a

---

[30] Complementarianism. (Accessed 2023, June 5) in *Wikipedia.* https://en.wikipedia.org/wiki/Complementarianism.

prophet and judge found in the book of Judges, confirms this and is further corroborated by the record of ten other female prophets or prophetesses.

"The housewife myth." Contrary to popular belief, the Old Testament does not relegate or limit women to being *'just housewives.'* This fact is substantiated in the fascinating account of Deborah's roles as prophetess and judge in Israel during the 12th century B.C. Moses delivered Israel from Pharoah, and he was succeeded by Joshua. After Joshua came Deborah, a woman, the third in the line of these great leaders, securing a signal victory over the enemies of Israel.

"The seductive myth." Some have caricatured women in the Old Testament as temptresses, seductresses, and morally and intellectually deficient. Women have often been blamed for the weakness of men and their downfall. This chapter lifts the narratives of women that counter these negative stereotypes and cites women of valour who left an indelible mark of excellence on the leadership fabric of home and society. This chapter refutes the notion that women should neither speak nor exercise authority.

Chapter 3. Jesus and Women: Women in the New Testament review how Jesus fought for a fair society and expressed great interest in women and children. When Jesus was on earth, many women followed him, these women were there with Jesus throughout his life; at his crucifixion; at his burial and were the first to see the empty tomb and the resurrected Christ. It was a woman who was first commissioned to announce the resurrection of Jesus. The Church today would do well to follow Jesus in giving women their value and an equal place.

Women were often among the marginalised, the ostracised, and the victimised of his day. A witness was commonly used in everyday life, however, according to Jewish convention, female witnesses were on the list of persons who were not competent to testify. Women were also forbidden to speak publicly to a male. The Talmud, (commonly referred to as a compilation of ancient teachings regarded as sacred and normative by Jews) suggested that a woman's place was in the home and that a man was not allowed to speak to a woman in public. It is against this backdrop that we can better appreciate Jesus's positive and restorative interaction with women, especially publicly.

Jesus's first post-resurrection appearance was to a woman, not to angels or apostles; not to the faithful Joseph or the true-hearted Nicodemus; but to a woman! And not the noblest of women, but Mary, out of whom he cast seven devils! *"Now when Jesus was risen early the first day of the week, he appeared first to Mary Magdalene, out of whom he had cast seven devils."* Mark 16:9. Jesus placed a high value on women without reference to class or status. He further gave women back their voice as recorded in Mark 16:7, 10, when the angel said to Mary, "But go, tell his disciples and Peter, 'He is going ahead of you into Galilee. There you will see him, just as he told you." "She went and told them that had been with him, as they mourned and wept". Verse 11 states: "And they when they heard that he was alive, and had seen of her, disbelieved." The angel's words "But go, tell his disciples and Peter" is a direct commission that gave the woman voice or agency as a witness, to the consternation of the disciples.

Why would Jesus risk commissioning this incredible story to a woman who was not considered a witness? And of all women, one with a questionable background? What a paradox! In a society where women were forbidden to be witnesses, Jesus gave women back their voice and commissioned them to "go into the entire world and preach the gospel". Jesus never silenced women; he empowered them even when it meant going against the conventions of his day. Churches, religious organizations and society will do well to follow Jesus's positive action. Jesus also gave women visibility or prominence. He left a memorial to women when He declared in Matthew 26:13, "Verily I say unto you, wheresoever this gospel shall be preached in the whole world, *there* shall also this, that this woman hath done, be told for a memorial of her." This is incredible!

The way Jesus empowered women and interacted with women at different strata in society becomes an interpretive lens through which the Church should interpret the scriptures which on the surface appear to silence women. We

should ask the question, what did Jesus do?

The Four Gospels allow us to examine the paradigm shift Jesus introduced on how women ought to be perceived and treated. The message of the kingdom of God was counter to the conventions of Jesus's day on how women were treated. Jesus taught *much through* parables; "But without a parable spake he not unto them: and when they were alone, he expounded all things to his disciples". Mark 4:34. Throughout the Gospels, Epistles, and the Apocalypse, women are elevated to such a high place that they are considered the Bride of God, Wise Virgins, the Pure Church, and likened to the kingdom of God. These sayings 2,000 years ago were quite affirmative and radical.

Jesus's interest in, and value for women lies at the very core of a happy home and stable society. Robbing a woman of her value upsets God and society. The value of women in the plan of God is indispensable. God placed a high value on women when he created them in his image. A marriage counsellor once said in a session, "Happy wife, happy life."[31] By extension, happy home, happy life; happy women, happy society. If you upset the God-given ideal for women and men in relationships, the home, church, and society will pay a hefty price.

Without doctrine or theological argument, Jesus liberated and elevated women, giving them *Value, Visibility, and Voice.* Jesus's treatment of women answers the questions about the roles of women, after the fall.

Chapter 4. Silence and Submission? Was St. Paul a Misogynist? (Someone with a prejudice against women) This chapter generates answers to the many questions raised on St. Paul's statements about women such as:

- What did St. Paul mean when he said, "Let the women keep silent in the churches" and, "But I suffer not a woman to teach, nor to usurp authority over the man, but to be in silence." and "Wives, submit yourselves unto your husbands, as unto the

---

[31] Pastor Leslie Moses, Marital counselling session (June 22, 2011), Deane Street, St Augustine, Trinidad & Tobago.

Lord." What did he mean?

- Were St. Paul's prohibitions of silence and submission in 1 Corinthians 14:34-35 localised or universal, applicable to married women only, or single women inside and outside the church?

- When St. Paul said it was unlawful for a woman to speak and disgraceful to speak in the church, what could he have meant and to whom was he speaking and what was the context? Were St. Paul's letters, Letters of Occasion, intended for a particular context or letters to be applied universally?

- What about St. Paul's commendation to women and his exhortation for them to cover their heads when praying and prophesying publicly, was he contradicting himself when he said that women should keep silent in the churches, yet permit them to prophesy and pray publicly?

- Did St. Paul truly mean that women should not speak and exercise authority when he recommended and appointed women in the churches? Did he contradict the scriptures which acknowledge at least ten godly women to whom God gave the gift of leadership, as prophets?

- What did St. Paul mean when he said, "There is neither Jew nor Gentile, bond nor free, male or female, but we are all one in Christ?"

- St. Paul spoke about gifts that the Holy Spirit gives to the church, did he state that any of them were gender-based, or rather, did he not say that the gifts were distributed to whomsoever God wills, male and female alike, a fulfilment of the prophet Joel in chapter 2:27, 28?

St. Paul would be astonished to know that a letter he wrote to the church of Ephesus in AD 62 would be applied to a congregation in Johannesburg, London, or New York in 2025, without extrapolating the *Sitz im Leben* or life setting of the text. The Apostle wrote letters to individual churches because counsels he gave to one church i.e., Ephesus, would not apply

to the church in Colossae, and vice versa. If we take his statements out of their immediate contexts and group them all it would appear that he is saying different things at different times, and yes, that's exactly what he did, he said different things at different times to different audiences, but he never contradicted himself. That's why he wrote Letters of Occasion, to recognise the individual nature of each situation; otherwise, in today's practice he would have simply copied and pasted the contents of each letter to all the churches, but he did not do that. Although each of St. Paul's letters begins with "grace and peace", we see that the content of each letter to each church is different.

We conclude that deciphering what St. Paul said about women is a hermeneutical issue: one of interpreting the scriptures. The said same St. Paul, instructed his protégé Timothy to "Rightly divide the word of truth". This chapter does just that: the work of exegesis and hermeneutics, ("Rightly dividing the word of truth.") The Church's failure to do this, in the main, has contributed to the widespread demeaning way women are seen and treated. Various narratives about women confirm that women were not muted but given a voice, neither were they as persons without authority, rather, they like men received direct communication from God and taught and led based on their divine calling.

St. Paul was not a misogynist; on the contrary, a protagonist for women. His statements when rightly interpreted empower women and not limit them.

Chapter 5. Ordination: Gendered privileges and spaces

The Oxymoron: Called by God but not ordained by men. This book would have cheated women and men if it did not give due theological thought and diligence to *the 'hot potato' of* women's ordination: the endorsement by the church for the full participation of women in ministry. In many Christian denominations and churches, women do the same work as men but are not given the same rights, privileges, and recognition. Women are excluded from a seat around the decision-making tables and certain positions of authority. (The argument used is that they are not ordained, when in fact, what is meant is that females are barred from certain positions of authority because St. Paul's instructions that women are to keep silent in the churches and not teach or exercise authority are universal commands to all women, for all times.) Of course, auxiliary statements by St. Paul are further used to argue this position.

This chapter sets out the etymology of the troubled word – ordination, which appears to be an exclusive masculine ordinance. We will look at the anomaly of women's exclusion from the ordained clergy of churches simply because they are female. However, before we talk about ordination in the church, we must understand the context in which ordination occurs; therefore, we need to briefly discuss the nature and function of the church: an inclusive body, with no walls or partitions. Joel 2:28 and Galatians 3:28.

When I say the church, I mean, not two entities of clergy and laity, but Laos: the body of Christ; the priesthood of all believers with Christ as head, and the Holy Spirit, equipping each member with spiritual gifts. We will explore ordination in the Bible, the Christian Church, and my denomination, the Seventh-day Adventist Church.

A faulty theology of women is the root of a misleading theology of ordination.

God's assignment to both males and females in the Garden of Eden was to have mutual dominion over the earth, and dominion is authority. God gave women authority in the beginning, and I dare say, there is no record of him taking it back. Why can women do everything a man does within the church, including being a minister, but not be considered suitable to be ordained? How do we explain the practice in some denominations of ordaining women as elders and deacons but not as pastors? Please explain on what theological grounds the church has taken its position and what the word ordination means.

In the Protestant world, the position that a woman should not be ordained seems to be predicated on St. Paul's injunction for a woman not to teach or exercise authority, compounded by the arguments of an ontological difference between male and female at creation or at worse, that a woman's subordination to a man is as a result of her role in the entrance of sin in the world. Hence, women are permanently relegated to subservience to men.

In the Roman Catholic tradition, a female cannot assume the role of the priest because ontologically, or by nature or gender, she cannot assume the role of representing Jesus who was male. (The representational function is strongly linked to the whole concept of the mass, where the emblem of the bread literally becomes the body of Christ-Transubstantiation) However, the gospel of St. John in chapter 1:14 makes it clear that Jesus became flesh. The Greek word used for flesh does not refer to either male or female, it simply means that Jesus became human. I must hasten to say that it was not Jesus's gender that saved us; it was not his masculinity that saved us or his femininity. Rather it was his divinity and sinlessness.[32]

In my tradition the Seventh-day Adventist Church, women are not ordained in ministry as their male counter paths. However, two resolutions were made to the General Conference of Seventh-day Adventists in 1881 and 1888 by eminent leaders of the church for women to be ordained. Mrs. Ellen G. White, one of the most prolific American female authors of the 19th and 20th centuries and co-founder of the movement supported the resolutions which read:

1.   Resolved: That all candidates for license and ordination should be examined with reference to their intellectual and spiritual fitness for the successful discharge of the duties which will devolve upon them as licentiates and ordained ministers. (No reference to gender)

2.   Resolved: That females possessing the necessary qualifications to fill that position, may, with perfect propriety, be

---

[32] Pierce and Groothuis, pp. 280-281.

set apart by ordination to the work of the Christian ministry.[33]

In one of her statements, Mrs. White said, "There are women who should labour in the gospel ministry. In many respects they would do better than the ministers who neglect to visit the flock of God…women who do such labour, especially full-time, were to be paid fairly for their work from the tithe. The tithe should go to those who labour in word and doctrine, be they men or women." She added: "Seventh-day Adventists are not in any way to belittle woman's work."[34]

Could you imagine the conviction that drove a statement like the above, 135 years ago? She further postulated, **"This question is not for men to settle. The Lord has settled it. You are to do your duty to the women who labour in the gospel**, whose work testifies that they are essential to carrying the truth into families. Their work is just the work that must be done and should be encouraged. **In many respects, a woman can impart knowledge to her sisters that a man cannot. The cause would suffer great loss without this kind of labour by women. Again, and again the Lord has shown me that women teachers are just as greatly needed to do the work to which He has appointed them as are men.**"[35] Mrs. White further asserted "It is the accompaniment of the Holy Spirit of God that prepares workers, both men and women, to become pastors to the flock of God."[36] The **determinant is not gender but evidence of the Holy Spirit.** To think that such declarations on equality and gender inclusiveness were emphatically stated well over a century ago is remarkable. Awesome indeed! No doubt, Mrs. White's comments were predicated on the authority of scripture Joel 2:28, Galatians 3:28, 1 Corinthians 12:11, Titus 2:11, and her personal convictions from God.

---

[33] (http://www.adventistarchives.org/docs/GCB/ GCB1863-88.pdf#view=fit) (Accessed August, 23, 2016).
[34] http://www.adventistarchives.org/docs/GCB/GCB1863-88.pdf#view=fit) (Accessed August, 23, 2016).
[35] Ellen Gould White, Evangelism, p. 493.
[36] Ellen Gould White, Gospel Workers, (1915 ed.) p. 96. (Accessed August 16, 2016).

The scriptures are clear, God calls both women and men alike and apportions His gifts to each one individually, as He wills, without regard to gender. God said to Jeremiah **"Before I formed thee in the belly, I knew thee; and before thou camest forth out of the womb I sanctified thee, and I ordained thee a prophet unto the nations."** (Jeremiah 1:5) Ordination is not a sacrament that the church grants to males that it deems worthy, ordination is God's calling in the life of a believer through his omniscience, be they female or male.

Conclusion.

The author sympathises with readers who, in their sincerity to be faithful to the inspiration of the scriptures, failed to do proper exegesis and hermeneutics and settled for a surface reading of the scriptures, which suggests a less than equal place for women. However, the accumulation of evidence renders St. Paul's controversial statements about women as Letters of Occasion addressed locally to specific situations and not intended to be universally applied or used to discriminate against women.

St. Paul's deployment and positive recommendation of notable women in the New Testament, support the view of the rest of the scriptures, that the calling, gifts, and commissioning of God are genderless: without regard to gender. The Apostle Paul fought for the freedoms and privileges of women, that they are included and not excluded in the work of the church.

Martin Luther King Jr. said, *"Injustice anywhere, is a threat to justice everywhere",* including the church. What we fail to condemn, we condone. There should be no discrimination in the church or society. Gender discrimination in the church or any other religious organisation is just as or even crueler than racial or economic discrimination. The church must not allow those who have been created in *the image of God* to be discriminated against, in the name of God, in the house of God and society. Gender is not choice, but design. If God so willed (male and female) and gifted them without regard to gender, why would the church discriminate against women?

Justice for Women: The Cry to End the Pandemic of Discrimination, Intimidation, Misogyny, Abuse and Violence against Women in Society and Religious Communities **calls the Christian Church to right the wrong of discriminating against women by interpreting the Bible contextually and taking a stand, not on culture, but on scripture. The Church must be true to the scriptures and "Rightly divide the word of truth" After all, the gospel of the kingdom is the Good News that men and women were equally created in the image and likeness of God in which there is no hierarchy and redeemed by his vicarious sacrifice. These facts place an inestimable value on both men and women equally. The Church, of all institutions on earth, has the theological framework to develop a theology about women that promotes a woman's God-ordained worth and equality**.

This publication concludes that reversing the trend of misogyny, patriarchy, inequality, and discrimination against women must begin upstream at the source: the ill-use of the Bible in producing a faulty theology about women, peddled by a patriarchal and misogynistic religious culture, authoritatively practiced in the name of God.

Men, I appeal to you, just as male philosophers and Church Fathers were very instrumental in peddling philosophies and theologies that discriminate against women, that men also take the responsibility to advocate for women's Value, Voice, Visibility, and Vocational calling. I appeal to every woman to acknowledge their uniqueness and value as they stand united and confident in the equality and purpose that God has ordained for women.

Madeleine Albright's words "**There** is a **special place** in **hell** for **women** who don't help other **women**", express the strength of conviction on the necessity for women {and men} to advocate for a level playing field for women.

In today's global village, class, race, nationality, gender, education, and other socio-economic barometers play a role in defining who people are, however, St. Paul was very unambiguous when he said, *"There is neither Jew nor Greek, slave nor free, male nor female, for **you are all one in Christ Jesus"*** Galatians 3:28 – KJV.

CHAPTER 1
The Genesis of Gender: Created Equal

"Equality is not a concept. It's not something we should be striving for. It's a necessity. Equality is like gravity. We need it to stand on this earth as men and women, and the misogyny that is in every culture is not a true part of the human condition. It is life out of balance, and that imbalance is sucking something out of the soul of every man and woman who's confronted with it. We need equality. Kinda now."—Joss Whedon.

Synopsis

The Genesis account does not leave any room for bias against women because of their gender. "The Bible affirms the equality of human worth and human rights between women and men; whatever human rights there may be, they belong no less to women than to men."[37]

Explore six truths that refute the justification for patriarchy, misogyny, and the limitation of women.

1. Ontology or the nature of woman: that woman was created in the image of God just as man was. In the image of God is characteristic of their essence: love, oneness and, equality.
2. Pre-eminence: that Adam was created first did not constitute an ontological or qualitative advantage over Eve. First, in this context is to do with order in time, not quality. (As a matter of fact, humanly speaking, we tend to improve on the first).
3. Co-dominion: helpmeet: that the woman as a helpmeet did not mean someone inferior to the first or an addendum, but rather, "one equal to, having the same authority as the other" reflecting the image of God, who are each the same and equal. The first man and woman were jointly given dominion or co-dominion over the earth. (Not domination over each other).
4. Co-culpability: that the woman and man were both culpable and responsible for the entrance of sin into the world (the fall) and the woman was not more culpable.
5. Co-Punishment: that punishment for the first woman's (Eve) role in the fall was equally matched with Adam's, and not a one-sided permanent sentence of subordination on all women. The Bible teaches that Eve was deceived, and Adam calculatedly transgressed, but God jointly punished them. If any of the pair should have been punished more, it should

---

[37] Pierce, Ronald W. Groothuis, Rebecca Merrill Fee, Gordon D. p. 306.

have been Adam, because he consciously and premeditatedly made a wrong decision.

6. **Co-redemption:** The woman was pardoned for her role in the fall and granted complete absolution as the man. Was she singled out for eternal torment by being subjected to permanent subordination to men? No, God provided a covering for Adam and Eve, and both were redeemed by the same sacrifice.

Equality in Genesis

At the core of the gender debate, are two of St. Paul's in-junctions. One cites the creation order in Genesis, and the other the entrance of sin into the world (the fall) as grounds to limit women. 1. "But I suffer not a woman to teach, nor to usurp authority over the man, but to be in silence. For Adam was first formed, then Eve". 1 Timothy 2:12. 2. "Adam was not deceived, but the woman being deceived was in the transgression". 1 Timothy 2:13-14. Consequently, many theologians and denominations justify their position of male headship on the mistaken notion of male pre-eminence: that Adam was created first, and the culpability of Eve's role in the fall.

Women and men experience things differently, it does not mean that one is superior or inferior to the other; it simply means that each is made for a purpose. "We acknowledge that due to cultural and biological factors, there are some generalised differences in behaviour between women and men, however, these differences do not warrant the traditional notion that women are deficient in rationality and are suited to be in subordination to men, rather these differences are ways in which women and men can complement one another as they live and work together."[38]

These differences are part of God's design, "Male and female He created them: In the image of God created he them." The Image of God or his likeness constitutes love, oneness, and equality. There is no hierarchy in the Godhead. Therefore, if male and female were made in

---

[38] Ibid., p. 307.

his image, it means that love, oneness, and equality are the patents of human beings, that's the watermark of interpersonal relationships setting humans apart from other creatures in God's creation. Human beings were made to reflect the image of God.

"If women and men are both fully human then women and men share equally in the distinctively human capacities, therefore, no woman can be deemed inferior to man solely on account of her womanhood."[39] Being female was not a choice, but God's design.

The Genesis account in chapter 1:27 says, "So God created man in his own image, in the image of God created he him; male and female created he them." A quick exegesis of this verse is important. Please note, "the use of the pronouns *us* and *our,* which are plural to identify the one speaking. The one speaking *(God the Father),* is in a relationship with others *(God the Son and Holy Spirit)* and is about to create in their image. "In his image", the image of God, is the stamp of the unity of three persons-oneness and equality."[40]

Hence, when Jesus was on earth, he said to Phillip, 'he that hath seen me hath seen the Father" (John 14:9), expressing the oneness and equality that is characteristic of the Godhead. Jesus is referred to as 'the express image of {God}", Hebrews 1:3. "In the image of God" means oneness and equality.

Complementarians postulate that women were created equal but were consequently placed in a position of subordination because of their role in the fall. Complementarians believe in Ontological equality, but not functional equality. [41]

Samuel Bacchiocchi falls into this group, he said, "The woman is equal to man because she is made of the same substance of Adam's body and is taken from his side to be his equal. Yet the woman is subordinate to man because she is created second and from and for

---

[39] Ibid., p. 307.

[40] Pierce, Ronald W. Groothuis, Rebecca Merrill Fee, Gordon D. p.80.

[41] Ibid, pp, 305-307.

man."[42] The use of the word 'subordinate' in this context is controversial and inflammatory, implying servitude. I can accept functional subordination (which was voluntary and not prescribed) if you want to use such a strong term, but not ontological subordination. **Jesus for instance, subordinated himself to the Father functionally to come as a son or human, but ontologically, He was equally God, his nature did not change**. Some Complementarians insist not only on functional subordination but ontological subordination, they say a woman by design, is made to be subordinate.

Bacchiocchi contends further, "Men and women are equal before God by virtue of creation and redemption. Yet God assigned distinctive and complementary roles for men and women to fill in their relation to each other. These roles are not nullified but clarified by Christ's redemption and should be reflected in the church."[43] 'Distinctive' roles as a differentiating mark of rank can give rise to ideologies that lead to discrimination, inequality and subordination. Bacchiocchi's position is referred to today as evangelical patriarchy, supporting equality of creation but inequality of roles. This distinction between being and roles is often the argument used to substantiate male headship and female submission.

There is another group known as Egalitarians who believe in the equality of males and females at creation and equality of roles. Broadly speaking, the views in this book fall into this category which challenges the arguments tendered by Complementarians and others to limit women.

Hermeneutically speaking, the view that man's creation before the woman implies his authority over her, cannot be substantiated by the study of the scripture in Genesis 1 and 2.

The pre-eminence argument
Pre-eminence does not equal superiority. The type of logic that can seek

---

[42] Samuele Bacchiocchi," Women in the Church: A Biblical Study on the Role of Women in the Church" (BIBLICAL PERSPECTIVES, Berrien Springs, Michigan, 1987), p. 29.
[43] Ibid, p. 93.

to find biblical justification for the subordination of women throughout the ages sounds too familiar and is dangerous. In the same vein, was the misuse of the Bible to sanction slavery.

Even though Eve was taken from Adam's rib, the Bible is expressly clear that she was not made in the image of Adam. The image is not to do with gender or form but essence or characteristic, because God is a Spirit, neither male nor female. Pierce and Groothuis expand on this viewpoint beautifully in their book – 'Discovering Biblical Equality: Complimentary Without Hierarchy'. They highlight that although masculine pronouns are often used to describe God, feminine and neuter ones are also used, e.g., 'hen', 'Ruach', and 'mother.'[44]

At creation, God (Elohim representing the Godhead) created human beings – both male and female, in their image. *"And God said, Let us make man in our image, after our likeness..."* Genesis 1:26. Was there any hint or suggestion of an ontological difference or qualitative difference between Adam and Eve, because one was male and the other female? Absolutely not; no ontological difference in God's creation was implied.

Some argue that Adam being created first and Eve second, implies that first connotes a quality of superiority. Many complementarians use the argument of pre-eminence to substantiate male headship. Adam created first is not a statement of superiority, Adam was not in a contest. First, has to do with the sequence in time, not a statement of ontology or quality. Neither at creation nor after the fall was a woman made inferior or less than her male counterpart. We cannot formulate a teaching on the word "first" to mean superior. According to the creation account, first, there was nothing, then light, water, plant life, and animals, then Adam, and finally, Eve. First and second in this context have to do with chronology, timing or sequence, not ontology or nature; else, according to the creation account, humans who were created on the sixth day would certainly be inferior to animals, nature and the rest of creation. First does not constitute an ontological advantage.

---

[44] Pierce, Ronald W. Groothuis, Rebecca Merrill Fee, Gordon D. pp. 296-297.

According to Rebecca Merrill Groothuis, "That man and woman were created sequentially in Genesis 2, may well be to demonstrate the need that they have for each other rather than to justify an implicit hierarchy or make a statement of quality."[45] The reasoning that Adam being created first connotes superiority, and Eve being created second as a helpmeet implies inferiority, is an illegitimate argument to substantiate the inequality between males and females.

Here is what a Bible commentator has to say on pre-eminence from the Master himself, "Again and again Jesus had tried to establish this principle among His disciples. When James and John made their request for pre-eminence, He had said, "Whosoever will be great among you, let him be your servant." Matthew 20:26. In My kingdom the principle of preference and supremacy has no place. The only greatness is the greatness of humility. The only distinction is found in devotion to the service of others."[46] Jesus himself taught, "So it is. Everyone who is now last will be first, and everyone who is first will be last." Matthew 20:16.

In the creation account of Genesis, the Sabbath is the seventh day chronologically, and it is set aside as being more special than the previous six days of creation because God blessed and sanctified the seventh day. (Genesis 2:3). First, second, third, fourth, fifth, sixth, seventh or any other numbers are not statements of quality necessarily, but determinants of time. We cannot formulate a teaching of pre-eminence as a statement of superiority based on sequence.

According to Dr Kristine Henrikson Garroway, "In biblical and ancient Near Eastern law, the firstborn son (,רוכב bəkôr) held a privileged position and received the birthright (,הרוכב bəkōrāh). Although this is not always the case in the Bible. We know from other ancient Near Eastern societies that the firstborn son had certain obligations as well,

[45] Rebecca Merrill Groothius, Good News for Women: A biblical picture of gender equality (Grand Rapids, Michigan: Baker, 1997), p. 137.
[46] White, E. G. "The Desire of Ages" Review and Herald Publishing Association, Washington DC, 1905, p. 350.

including responsibilities upon the death of his father."[47] To use the primogeniture argument to substantiate the inequality between male and female at creation is not a consistent hermeneutical argument because "there are examples in scripture where the birthright did not go to the firstborn or where it was forfeited. i.e., Genesis 25 (Jacob and Esau) Jacob's two sons, Reuben and Joseph."[48] Simri, the son of Hosah was made chief although he was not the firstborn. 1 Chronicles 26:10.

"A helpmeet for him"

Another passage we need to exegete or interpret is Genesis 2:18, "And the LORD God said, it is not good that the man should be alone; I will make him a helpmeet for him." "The designation of the woman as a helpmeet to the man in Genesis 2 has evoked much discussion."[49] and is of primary interest to the discussion about the role of women. The traditional reading of "helpmeet" must refer to someone who is in a subordinate position."[50] Someone who aids. On the contrary, the Hebrew word "Ezer" for helpmeet clarifies any ambiguity about a woman's role. It means "one who is the same as the other and who surrounds, protects, aids, helps, supports."[51]

> If one looks at the other usage of the word *Ezer* in the scripture, one will see that Ezer refers to either God or military allies. In all other cases, the one giving the help is superior to the one receiving the help. Adding *kenegdo* (meet) modifies the meaning to that of equal rather than superior status. Scripture is so awesome. God says just what He means. Dr Susan Hyatt gives the following definition from her book ``In the *Spirit We're Equal* "Re: Hebrew ezer *kenegdo.* In Genesis 2:18, the word "helpmeet" does not occur. The Hebrew expression *ezer kenegdo* appears, meaning "one who is the same as the other and who surrounds, protects, aids, helps,

---

[47] Jeffrey Tigay, *The JPS Torah Commentary: Deuteronomy* (Philadelphia: Jewish Publication Society, 1996), 196.

[48] Pierce, Ronald W. Groothuis, Rebecca Merrill Fee, Gordon D. p. 84.

[49] Pierce, Ronald W. Groothuis, Rebecca Merrill Fee, Gordon D. p. 86.

[50] Ibid., p. 86.

[51] https://godswordtowomen.org/help.htm. (Accessed September 12, 2022).

supports." There is no indication of inferiority or a secondary position in a hierarchical separation of the male and female "spheres" of responsibility, authority, or social position. The word *ezer* is used twice in the Old Testament to refer to the female and 14 times to refer to God. For example, in the Psalms when David says, "The Lord is my Helper, he uses the word *ezer*."[52]

"The noun `*Ezer* occurs twenty-one times in the Old Testament. In many of the passages, it is used in parallelism to words that denote strength or power. Some examples are: "There is none like the God of Jeshurun, The Rider of the Heavens in your strength (`-z-r), and on the clouds in his majesty." (Deut. 33:26, [author's] translation).

"Blessed are you, O Israel! Who is like you, a people saved by the Lord? He is the shield of your strength (`-z-r) and the sword of your majesty." (Deut. 33:29, [author's] translation)

The case that begins to build is that we can be sure that `*Ezer* means "strength" or "power" whenever it is used in parallel with words for majesty or other words for power such as `*oz* or `*uzzo*. The presence of two names for one king, Azariah and Uzziah, both referring to God's strength, makes it abundantly clear that the root `*ezer* meaning "strength" was known in Hebrew.

Therefore, could we conclude that Genesis 2:18 be translated as "I will make a power [or strength] corresponding to man." Freedman even suggests based on later Hebrew that the second word in the Hebrew expression found in this verse should be rendered equal to him. If so, then God makes for the man a woman fully his equal and fully his match. In this way, the man's loneliness will be assuaged.

This line of reasoning, which stresses full equality, is continued

---

[52] https://godswordtowomen.org/help.htm. (Accessed September 12, 2022).

in Genesis 2:23 where Adam says of Eve, "This is now bone of my bones and flesh of my flesh; she shall be called 'woman,' for she was taken out of man." The idiomatic sense of this phrase "bone of my bones" is a "very close relative" or analogous to "one of us" or in effect "our equal."[53] The woman was made for a purpose. This does not convey inferiority.

"The solution to man's loneliness is found in the creation of the woman who God built from Adam's side. The term is used for the side of the ark and of the tabernacle in Exodus 25:12,14, representing a constituent part of the man that is used for the woman. A basic building pattern that can be drawn from man and used to create a second person like the first...This is borne out in Adam's words, "bone of my bone and flesh of My Flesh", and affirmation of equality."[54]

Mrs. White, author and biblical commentator had this to say, "Eve was created from a rib taken from the side of Adam, signifying that she was not to control him as the head, nor to be trampled under his feet as an inferior, but to stand by his side as an equal, to be loved and protected by him."[55] There's no hint or suggestion of inferiority in the creation of women. **God did not give Adam an inferior person to compliment him.** Bacchiocchi's argument about submission does not stand. His comments are also espoused by the group known as patriarchists. "Patriarchists consign women to a permanently inferior status in a hierarchy of spiritual authority, calling, responsibility and privilege, all the while insisting that women are not spiritually inferior to men."[56]

According to Sharon Platt McDonald, "We need no longer say the old adage, behind every good man, there is a good woman, she is not behind, but beside him. We must now say, beside every good man, is a

[3] Ibid.
[4] Pierce, Ronald W. Groothuis, Rebecca Merrill Fee, Gordon D. p. 86-87.
[5] Ellen G. White, *Evangelism* (Washington, D.C., 1946), p. 472.

[5] Pierce, Ronald W. Groothuis, Rebecca Merrill Fee, Gordon D. p. 314.

good woman."[57]

2. Co-dominion not domination

Adam and Eve were given dominion over the creatures and the environment, not over one another. Sin brought dysfunction and imbalance in nature and human relationships, and consequently, domination, force and power struggles. We saw mankind trying to dominate one another; in Eden, Cain killed his brother Abel, with whom he should have lived as an equal.

"As the sun and moon rule over day and night so through its multiplication humanity rules over the earth by its presence throughout the world."[58] Dominion sets Adam and Eve apart from everything else that was created.[59] This dominion that was given to both Adam and Eve, was not altered with the entrance of sin which followed in succeeding chapters. The male and femaleness of Adam can be seen in the light of the coming assignment of fertility and dominion; to be like their creator in being able to procreate and have dominion, to multiply and replenish the earth.[60] "While the animals were capable of procreating, Adam and Eve as humans would be different from the creation by having the image of God and the role of dominion."[61]

"In its narrative, Genesis 1 declares that God and no other deity created the universe, while Genesis 2 explains humanity's special relationship with God and explores the harmonious relationship that he enjoyed with his God, his work, his world and his partner. In Genesis 2, the man is given responsibility for the garden, a responsibility that was already given to both man and woman in Genesis 1 but he is not given authority over the woman. Genesis nowhere suggests a hierarchical relationship between the man and the woman and certainly not because of the order of creation."[62]

---

[57] Sharon-Platt McDonald, quoted in a face-to-face conversation, Watford, England, June 2022.
[58] Pierce, Groothuis, p. 81.
[59] Ibid., p. 81.
[60] Ibid., p. 81.
[61] Ibid., p. 81.
[62] Ibid., p. 85.

The image of God in which we were created is a constant reminder for us to adjust not to the dysfunctional order of reality that we have inherited because of sin, but to seek God's original plan of oneness and equality. The Gospel, after all, is about the restoration of God's ideal and that includes the image of God in males and females. The image of God does not consist of a hierarchy; "For there are three that bear record in heaven, the Father, the Word, and the Holy Ghost: and these three are one." 1 John 5:7. Love manifested in unity and equality, constitutes the image of God.

3. Co-culpability

While we are in the Book of Genesis, let's address the underlying assumption that because of Eve's transgression in the Garden of Eden, she should be punished by being in subordination to her husband Adam, and not only Eve, but all women, even unmarried women must carry the consequence of permanent subordination to men in general, everywhere! Sounds like the teaching of eternal torment, that a loving God will only be appeased by seeing the rebellious burn forever, literally.

The issue of original sin, or the entrance of sin into the world, sometimes referred to as "the fall", does appear in the scriptures: "And the LORD God said to the woman, 'What is this you have done?' The woman said, 'The serpent deceived me, and I ate.'" Genesis 3:13. This acknowledgement by Eve is often cited as the justification for Eve and all other women to be eternally remembered and punished for woman's role in the entrance of sin. Let's examine the motif carefully, that all women were to be punished singly, punitively and indefinitely.

4. Co-Punishment

When God visited the couple in the Garden of Eden after they both ate the fruit, he did not call to Eve, nor did he singly punish her alone. To the contrary, God said, "Adam, where are you?" He Called on Adam as the accountability partner, Genesis 3:9. Secondly, both Adam and Eve were jointly held responsible. Adam was not deceived, which is confirmed in his reply to God: "And the man answered, "The woman whom You gave me, she gave me fruit from the tree, and I ate it".

Genesis 3:12. Adam knowingly ate the fruit. Adam could have chosen to stand up for what was right, but he knowingly and conscientiously didn't. Thirdly, both Adam and Eve were punished with parity; for Eve, the consequence was pain in childbirth; for Adam, the consequence was through the sweat of his brow, he would then have to till the soil. Please note that Adam and Eve were mutually guilty of bringing sin into the world and mutually suffered the consequences of their actions.

The Bible says Eve was deceived, unlike Adam, who consciously plunged the whole world into universal sin. He was the representative of humankind, not Eve. It was Adam's transgression that brought universal guilt; hence, God held him accountable. The inference is clear, if Eve had the foresight Adam had, probably, she would not have eaten the fruit. Therefore, if at all we want to establish culpability, the lot would fall on Adam and not Eve. **The question, "Adam, where art thou?" is still being asked of men today! Men, where are you? Where are you when women are at risk? Men, what are you doing about the injustices done to women? When men show up, life will be different for women and girls in our society.**

"He should rule over thee"

We must consider at this juncture God's words, "He should rule over thee" Genesis 3:16. Was this to be a punitive sentence, a bit of eternal punishment if you will, for Eve and domination of all other women by men? Was this prescriptive (This is how it ought to be) or descriptive? (This is how it would be) Did Eve's participation in the fall bring an eternal consequence to all women arbitrarily, even those who would not even be in a male-female relationship? No, "he should rule over thee" was descriptive because of the changes; the pulling and togging that transgression would make. Don't forget, Satan or the adversary of God, projects the opposite of God or stands in opposition to what God declares, that's why he is called the adversary: he hates oneness, unity and equality; he fosters, division, discord, disparity and inequality. If at all God was prescribing it, there must have been great wisdom in him assigning Adam to protect Eve, to be her accountability partner, (two is always better than one) to be present but not to dominate her. The context does not suggest domination, after all it was Adam's actions that permanently changed the human condition, not Eve's.(Romans 5:12 "Wherefore, as by one man sin entered into the world, and death by sin; and so death passed upon all men, for that all have sinned).

"The Hebrew verb to rule'kabash' and to dominate'radar', suggests the taking of the land and its stewardship as found in Joshua 18 vs 1. Stewardship is given to humanity male and female in God's command in Genesis 1 26 and 27."[63] Neither of these was reversed in the Fall but because of Eve's vulnerability, she would now have to consult with Adam. As a wife, she will be accountable to her husband. On her own, she will be vulnerable therefore she must check in with Adam. Another Hebrew word for rule can be interpreted, as "To deliver". Adam would serve as a deliverer or even judge, in other words, his presence will save Eve from future exposure to the enemy by being able to judge or assess the circumstances.

As the sun rules the day and the moon the night, "rule" has a function to guide, to give light to, illuminate or measure out. This concept is consistent with God's word "He shall rule over thee". Eve must no longer wander away from Adam nor Adam from her, instead, Adam would be responsible for ensuring that he guides or gives light to Eve's decisions and that his influence and presence will protect her well-being and safety. Interdependence and mutuality of action instead of independence and existential preference. (Consistent with St. Paul's counsel in Ephesians 5:21 "Submitting yourselves one to another in the fear of God" Mutual submission.

Adam's role of "ruling" was that of being present, shadowing, giving guidance or protecting his wife. This would involve greater accountability between them both. Basically, "he shall rule over thee" was God's way of saying, stay together or don't do anything without communicating with one another and yes, Adam must "rule" over his Eve, he must be present, not passive. Here is wisdom from Solomon found in Ecclesiastes 4:9,10 "Two are better than one; because they have a good reward for their labour. **10** For if they fall, the one will lift up his fellow: but woe to him that is alone when he falleth; for he hath

---

[63] Pierce, Ronald W. Groothuis, Rebecca Merrill Fee, Gordon D. pp. 81-82

not another to help him up". Wow! How apt? Yes, If Adam was with Eve, the narrative would have had a different ending.

5. Co-gratis...redemption.

Fourthly, both Adam and Eve were offered mercy, there was no separate type of atonement based on gender differences. There is no biblical or theological rationale for a two-pronged redemptive package. There was only one package for the redemption of both, Genesis 3:15, a promise of universal forgiveness. Gender was not a differentiating factor in creation, dominion or assignment, nor in the redemption of the couple. The plan of redemption is about restoring man's relationship with God and with each other. Jesus came to change our living conditions which the curse of sin brought. This is important because we don't have to carry out sinful practices and ways of living, we can aspire to, and achieve restoration because of God's mercy and power operating in our lives.

This chapter explores whether Adam and Eve were created equal or not. Nothing could change the fact that women were created in the image and likeness of God, equally as men. Men were not created with any ontological superiority over women, and neither were women demoted, sentenced or made less than a woman because of woman's role in the entrance of sin.

For those who argue for ontological equality at creation but role inequality because of sin, let me remind them that at the cross, Christ bought back everything that was lost in the fall. In conversation with the Pharisees about divorce, Jesus said **"Moses permitted you to divorce your wives because of your hardness of heart; but it was not this way from the beginning. 9. Now I tell you that whoever divorces his wife, except for sexual immorality, and marries another woman, commits adultery."**

There is a hermeneutical principle in Jesus's words that could be extrapolated and applied to the issue of women being placed in permanent submission because of sin. If we for a brief moment were to agree with Complementarians who argue for equality at creation but inequality in roles because of sin, Jesus's words can be interpreted here to say, even if sin brought negative consequences in the relationship between Adam and Eve, even if we interpret "rule over thee" literally, Jesus said, this description of what sin brought is not my ideal, "it was not this way from the beginning". This is not my ideal, I want you to go back to how it was in the beginning with ontological equality and role equality. This is what grace is all about, restoring unity, oneness, and equality that was God designed.

For those who may still want to argue for functional inequality because of sin, please take into consideration heaven's master plan, (the plan of redemption) to restore man's relationship with God and with each other. Jesus came into this world to do just that, to change the course of things brought on by the curse of sin. This is important because we don't have to carry out sinful practices and ways of living, we are no longer under the curse of the law, but under grace, therefore, we can aspire to, and achieve restoration from the attitudes and behaviours that are as a result of sin.

The Genesis account facilitates a theological understanding of the ontological equality of woman at creation; her functional equality of dominion over creation; her mutual culpability & punishment for sin, and her mutual redemption from the fall. A theological understanding of these issues lay the foundation for any future interpretation of other passages of the scriptures, be they on the nature, being, and status of both man and woman or the roles of women within the church, home and society.

6. No hierarchical difference between male and female

The hierarchy between males and females is theologically unsound. This concept has no origin in the creation narrative because there is no such in the Godhead. 1 John 5:7 says, "For there are three that bear record in heaven, the Father, the Word, and the Holy Ghost: **and these three are one." If therefore the three in heaven are one and equal, and male and female were made in the same image and likeness of God we can safely conclude that there is no hierarchy between males and females because hierarchy does not exist between the Father, the Word and the Holy Ghost in whose image, male and female were made.**

God's creation of a helpmeet for Adam as a solution to his need did not come in the form of an inferior person to him. The Hebrew word for **h**elpmeet, "Ezer" means "face to face", and "equal to" a phrase used of God who is our helper. Adam himself understood this very well for upon seeing Eve, he exclaimed, "This is now bone of my bone and flesh of my flesh", his statement, is an affirmation of Eve's equality."[64]

This chapter refutes the arguments of inequality and pre-eminence in creation, often inferred by misinterpreting St. Paul's reference to the creation order and women's role in the entrance of sin into the world, as grounds for the subordination of all women to men. We can therefore conclude this chapter having established a theology of women which will now become the arbitrator for interpreting other passages of the scriptures which may seem to infer a less-than-equal status for women.

---

[64] Ibid., p. 87.

CHAPTER 2
Called and Gifted: Women in the Old Testament

"When women are empowered, they immeasurably improve the lives of everyone around them—their families, their communities, and their countries. This is not just about women; we men need to recognise the part we play too. Real men treat women with dignity and give them the respect they deserve."— Prince Harry, Duke of Sussex.

Synopsis

The limitation of women in society is generally based on the theory that by nature, women are not equal to men and therefore should not share equally in roles of authority. Sin did not reverse God's calling and gifts to women, nor limit them. The Old Testament affirms women endowed by God with gifts and abilities which made room for their various assignments, including roles of authority. Even against the backdrop of what was considered a patriarchal society where women and children were often taken as property during war, inspiration did not fail to record the narratives of women in God-given positions of influence and authority.

Deborah's narrative as a prophet and judge, found in the book of Judges, is further corroborated by the record of ten other prophetesses, or women with authority. A prophet would often be given warnings or admonitions from God to the king, which were often treated as very authoritative.

This chapter addresses two burning questions in the debate on women, namely:
1. Does the Bible, frequently used to confirm patriarchy, silence or forbid women to speak?
2. Does the Bible forbid women from exercising authority?

The answers to these questions will put to rest the arguments upon which the case for a woman's silence and subordination are often predicated.

Women Called by God in the Old Testament

From beginning to end, both the Old and New Testaments incorporate women at the centre of God's plan. Even against the backdrop of a patriarchal society, women have been featured in significant places of authority throughout the scriptures. Many of these narratives, though not taught, are nonetheless very prominent in the biblical canon. Sadly, many women have been caricatured and portrayed as either temptresses or seducers and therefore responsible for the fall of Bible heroes like Sampson and David in the Bible. They are wrongly held responsible for men's actions and lust! We read of women like Delilah, Gomer and Jezebel, but there are many women of valour, whose gifts, including that of leadership, are immortalized in the scriptures. We think of women like Deborah, Miriam, Esther, Ruth, Naomi, the Queen of Sheba and the other four prophetesses in the Old Testament, not even to mention the many women in the New Testament like Dorcas, Lydia, Junia, Prescilla, Phillip's four daughters and Anna who were female prophets.

In the book of Proverbs, an entire chapter is dedicated to a poem about women. Lemuel's mother counsels him in Proverbs 31 on finding a woman of valour, one whose abilities exceed being successfully domesticated. "Who can find a virtuous woman? For her price is above rubies". (Proverbs 31:10).

The Woman of Noble Character

[10] A wife of noble character who can find?
She is worth far more than rubies.
11 Her husband has full confidence in her
and lacks nothing of value.
12 She brings him good, not harm, all
the days of her life.
13 She selects wool and flax
and works with eager hands. 14
She is like the merchant ships,
bringing her food from afar.
15 She gets up while it is still night;

she provides food for her family
and portions for her female servants.
16 She considers a field and buys it; out of
her earnings she plants a vineyard. 17 She
sets about her work vigorously;
her arms are strong for her tasks.
18 She sees that her trading is profitable,
and her lamp does not go out at night. 19
In her hand she holds the distaff and
grasps the spindle with her fingers. 20 She
opens her arms to the poor
and extends her hands to the needy.
21 When it snows, she has no fear for her household; for
all of them are clothed in scarlet.
22 She makes coverings for her bed;
she is clothed in fine linen and purple.
23 Her husband is respected at the city gate, where he
takes his seat among the elders of the land.

24 She makes linen garments and sells them,
and supplies the merchants with sashes.
25 She is clothed with strength and dignity;
she can laugh at the days to come.
26 She speaks with wisdom,
and faithful instruction is on her tongue.
27 She watches over the affairs of her household
and does not eat the bread of idleness. 28
Her children arise and call her blessed;
her husband also, and he praises her: 29
"Many women do noble things,
but she surpasses them all."
30 Charm is deceptive, and beauty is fleeting;
but a woman who fears the Lord, she is to be praised.
31 Honor her for all that her hands have done, and
let her works bring her praise at the city gate.

Every line in this acrostic carries the pronoun "she" or "her" for emphasis on the priceless value of the woman. What an elevated description of women, in stark contrast to the warped ones penned by influential Church Fathers and philosophers.

In Exodus 20:12, the Ten Commandments require children to "Honour thy father and thy mother". In what was considered a very patriarchal society, the fifth Commandment requires respect for both parents, the father being mentioned first in Exodus, however, in Leviticus 19:3, the mother is mentioned first. God said to Moses, say to the children of Israel "**Ye shall fear every man his mother, and his father, and keep my Sabbaths**: I am the LORD your God". Was this reversal of order coincidental? Absolutely not, we were not left to conclude that the woman comes second from a surface reading of the scriptures. **Proverbs 1:8 says "Listen, my son, to your father's instruction and do not forsake your mother's teaching".** Here we see **the role of the mother as a teacher** requiring honour in a patriarchal society. **(A woman should not speak? …" I suffer not a woman to teach"?)** One of the responsibilities of the Jewish mother was to teach her children the Torah or Law.

This chapter highlights the important role of women in the plan of God. Women of Valour were not exceptions but rather the rule. From the very beginning, God intended that women should reflect their (God's) image. Chapter 1 of this book showed that from the very onset of creation, women were created to have an equal part in God's plan. The Old Testament narratives about women confirm their influence in what was a very patriarchal society. God, through holy inspiration, did not fail to weave the narratives of women amongst the stories of men.

The narratives of women in the Old Testament are critical in formulating a theology of women which throws light on questions such as: Did God call and assign women to speak and exercise authority in the Old Testament?

The Greek word *Propheteuo* means "*to prophesy, to be a prophet, speak forth or to predict by divine inspiration, to utter forth or to declare a thing that could only be known by divine revelation.*" Acts 21:9. A prophet (male or female) is the mouthpiece for the one who sends him or her; the prophet speaks on behalf of the sender, Exodus 7:1-2. **The role of the prophet was to be God's** spokesperson, Amos 3:7: to prophecy or speak, and secondly, by that person speaking on behalf of God, their words were taken as the highest authority. God called women and gave them messages to speak. The fact that they were acknowledged as called by God was a stamp of authority.

The prophet Joel said, *"And it shall come to pass afterwards, that I will pour out my spirit upon all flesh, and your sons and your daughters shall prophesy. Joel 2:28.* "D*aughters shall prophesy"*, not one daughter as an exception but daughters-plural, equally as the sons, prophesying. *Israel's most powerful and influential leader was not the king or the priest, but the prophet. Their authority was not derived from their status or gender but from God.*

Eleven female prophets mentioned in the scriptures:

1. Miriam -

"And Miriam the prophetess, the sister of Aaron, took a timbrel in her hand; and all the women went out after her with timbrels and with dances. And Miriam answered them, Sing ye to the Lord, for he hath triumphed gloriously; the horse and his rider hath he thrown into the sea." Exodus 15:20-21

2. Noadiah-

"My God, think thou upon Tobiah and Sanballat according to these their works, and on the prophetess Noadiah, and the rest of the prophets, that would have put me in fear." Nehemiah 6:14

3. Huldah -

"So Hilkiah the priest, Ahikam, Achbor, Shaphan, and Asaiah went to Huldah the prophetess, the wife of Shallum the son of Tikvah, the son of Harhas, keeper of the wardrobe. She was a contemporary of the prophet Jeremiah, during the reign of King Josiah." 2 Kings 22:14

4. Isaiah's wife:

"And I went unto the prophetess; and she conceived and bare a son. Then said the Lord to me, Call his name Mahershalalhashbaz." Isaiah 8:1

5. Anna:

"And there was one Anna, a prophetess, the daughter of Phanuel, of the tribe of Aser: she was of a great age and had lived with a husband seven years from her virginity." Luke 2:36

6, 7, 8, 9. Philip's four daughters:

"And the next day we that were of Paul's company departed and came unto Caesarea: and we entered into the house of Philip the evangelist, which was one of the seven; and abode with him. And the same man had four daughters, virgins, which did prophesy." Acts 21:8-9

10. Jezebel:

"Notwithstanding I have a few things against thee, because thou sufferest that woman Jezebel, which calleth herself a prophetess, to teach and to seduce my servants to commit fornication, and to eat things sacrificed unto idols."

11. Deborah:

"Now Deborah, a prophetess, the wife of Lappidoth, was judging Israel at that time." Judges 4:4" [65]

Deborah an Old Testament "Shero"

Contrary to popular belief, the Old Testament does not relegate or limit women to being "just wives." This fact is substantiated

---

[65] https://www.neverthirsty.org/bible-qa/qa-archives/ question/prophetesses-in-the-bible/. (Accessed August 15, 2016).

in the story of Deborah's roles as prophet and judge in Israel during the 12th century B.C. who delivered Israel from the hands of Pharaoh. Deborah succeeded Joshua, after the death of Moses. The Book of Judges immortalises the captivating and stunning feats of Old Testament history through Deborah, a female leader of no mean calibre. We are all too familiar with the Old Testament heroes, Moses and Joshua. In this line-up, we see next, Deborah, standing tall in the succession of great leaders, securing a signal victory over the enemies of Israel. **God gave women divine approval and divine authority, equally, as he gave to men.** Inspiration has not failed to lift women and record stories of women of God, in God-given positions of power and influence. Did God command women to speak? Yes. Did God empower women to exercise authority? Yes.

Besides being a prophetess, Deborah was a judge. The Hebrew word for judge is "shaphat" which means "to deliver" or "to rule."[66] Certainly, Deborah was called by God to lead and exercise authority. As told in the book of Judges, 4:15:31, Deborah led the nation of Israel to a stunning victory over Israel's enemies. As a judge of Israel, Deborah would have a wide range of responsibilities, including deciding controversies, giving verdicts, and executing judgments. She is honourably called "a mother in Israel"; unlike some of the great heroes of the Bible like Moses, David and Sampson, there is no scandal or moral lapse associated with her.

Deborah's gender did not preclude her from the high offices of prophet and judge. Deborah was called and gifted because she had a special connection with God. It is not about gender but God's agenda, "This is the word of the LORD to Zerubbabel: `Not by might nor by power, **{or gender} but by my Spirit,' says the LORD Almighty." Zachariah 4:1. {Emphasis by author}. It is God who empowers humans to accomplish his purpose.**

---

[66] https://exploringthetruth.org/judges-essentials-lesson-notes. (Accessed August 15, 2022).

Deborah at war for the Israelites

During times of war and national conflict, women and girls are often taken as prisoners of war, they could expect to be captured, taken as spoil, raped, and killed. Hence the irony of the song in Judges Chapter 5, with poetic justice, Deborah depicts how a woman who would normally become a victim, was victor and the male enemies who would capture women were now being captured by a woman. Judges Chapter 5 in the heart of the Old Testament is an irrefutable defence against misogyny in the Bible.

"There is no indication that the men of Israel had any problem with the fact that she was a woman. They neither were shamed of her gender, nor did they fear that she had usurped a male-only position. The church could learn a thing or two from this biblical example. Interestingly, Deborah is the only judge that is portrayed in an entirely positive light."[67]

Today, we see examples of male and female leaders working side-by-side. For example – President Barack Obama and Secretary of State Hillary Clinton and President Joe Biden and Vice President Kamala Harris executing their leadership roles collaboratively. Likewise, we see Deborah doing the same for Barak in a time of crisis, as she accompanies him, and the battle is fought and won. Sisera is completely defeated. Interestingly, Deborah was the first and only female judge in the Bible. She made history. She was the first 'Shero,' coming after the great masculine biblical heroes.

A comparative analysis with modern-day Vice President Kamala Harris, sees her making history as a double first. The first female Vice President and the first Black woman in a position of this calibre. Kamala also served with distinction in the judiciary system, just as Deborah led as an outstanding judge.

Deborah could not only prophesy, arouse, rule, and fight but also write. It was said of Julius Caesar that, "he wrote with the same

---

[67] https://graceintorah.net/tag/the-song-of-deborah/. (Accessed October 17, 2022).

ability with which he fought." This observation can also be true of Deborah, who, after her victory over the Canaanites, composed a song which is regarded as one of the finest specimens of ancient Hebrew poetry, being superior to the celebrated song of Miriam. This song of praise, found in Judges Chapter 5, magnifies the Lord as being the One who enabled Israel's leaders to conquer their enemies. Edward Bulwer-Lytton said, "The pen is mightier than the sword". Deborah's song testifies that God will make your enemies your footstool.

Through the story of Deborah's victory over Jabin, we can attest that the gifts of God are without regard to gender. Judges Chapter 5 celebrates the magnanimous achievement through this woman, called and gifted to the leadership of Israel. The story concludes, "And the land had rest forty years." Judges 5:31. God's power through a woman.

Similarly, we see this in the book of Esther the role of another woman who made history, this time, not a prophet but a queen, Queen Esther. In Esther Chapters 5-9, see how the Jews were taunted and mistreated by Haman, and observe in God's providence how Esther, a Jewish woman, became instrumental in delivering the entire population of Jews and got justice. In *chapter 4:14 we read these famous words,* "For if thou altogether holdest thy peace at this time, *then* shall their enlargement and deliverance arise to the Jews from another place; but thou and thy father's house shall be destroyed: and who knoweth whether thou art come to the kingdom for *such* a time as this?

Certainly, whoever was being called upon to save an entire nation from extinction must have had to be a person in position and with influence, isn't this what authority is all about? It was not a coincidence but providence that Queen Esther was in a position to stop the genocide. (Haman was hung on the very gallows that he made for Mordecai. It is not about gender, or is it? If we stop at gender, we have missed the truth of the scriptures: "It is not by might or by power but by my spirit saith the Lord." Zach. 4:6. God positioned Esther to assume the role of deliverer for the Jews.

"It is not the capabilities you now possess, or ever will have, that will give you success. It is that which the Lord can do for you. We need to have far less confidence in what man can do and far more confidence in what God can do for every believing soul. He longs to have you reach after Him by faith. He longs to have you expect great things from Him. He longs to give you an understanding of temporal as well as spiritual matters. He can sharpen the intellect. He can give tact and skill. Put your talents into the work, ask God for wisdom, and it will be given to you."[68] God gives to whomsoever he wills.

The Old Testament is replete with case studies and theories that confirm a theology of women integral in the plan of God. The prophet Joel in the Old Testament declared, "And it shall come to pass afterward, that I will pour out my spirit upon all flesh; and your sons and your daughters shall prophesy, your old men shall dream dreams, your young men shall see visions". (Joel 2:28) God is no respecter of persons, and His calling and gifts are without regard to gender. Joel's words above are an endorsement of what God had already done through Deborah and other women, and not simply a prediction about the future.

The word of a prophet had authority because it was from God, not because of the gender of the one communicating.

The housewife myth. Contrary to popular belief, the Old Testament does not relegate or limit women to being '*just wives.*' This fact is substantiated in the fascinating account of Deborah's roles as prophetess and judge in Israel during the 12th century B.C. Moses delivered Israel from Pharoah, and he was succeeded by Joshua. After Joshua came Deborah, a woman, the third in the line of these great leaders, securing a signal victory over the enemies of Israel.

The seductive myth. Some have caricatured women in the Old Testament as temptresses, seductresses and morally and intellectually deficient. Women have often been blamed for the weakness of men and their downfall. This chapter lifts the

---

[68] Ellen G. White," Christ Object Lesson ", Review and Herald Publishing Association, Washington, D.C., [1941] p. 146.

narratives of women that counter these negative stereotypes and cites Women of Valor who have left an indelible mark of excellence on the leadership fabric of home and society. This chapter refutes the notion that women should neither speak nor exercise authority. Eleven women in the scriptures were identified as prophets. There is also Queen Esther, although not classified as a prophet, nonetheless, her decisive action and leadership saved the Jewish people from extermination.

The revelation in this chapter serves to broaden our perspective and help us to re-examine our views on inclusiveness and equality of opportunity, whether at home, in church, in religious organizations or in society. The Old Testament intentionally lifts women of valour. Women were not silenced or denied opportunities for leadership because of their gender. Quoting the scriptures out of their context to substantiate the teaching that women should not speak and or exercise authority is unbiblical. Narratives about women in the Bible serve as a hermeneutical lens through which we can interpret the few passages of the scriptures which on the surface may seem to suggest that women should be silent, not permitted to teach or hold positions of authority.

Ellen G. White, an American Bible commentator said over a century ago, "There are women who should labour in the gospel ministry. In many respects, they would do more good than the ministers who neglect to visit the flock of God." Women who do such labour, especially full-time, were to be paid fairly for their work from the tithe. "The tithe should go to those who labour in word and doctrine, be they, men or women." She added, "Seventh-day Adventists are not in any way to belittle woman's work."[69]

The same author added, "The minister and the church members are to unite as one person in labouring for the up-building and prosperity of the church. Everyone who is a true soldier in the army of the Lord will be an earnest, sincere, efficient worker,

---

[69] Evangelism. Review and Herald Publishing Association, Washington, D.C., [1941] p. 492.

labouring to advance the interests of Christ's kingdom."[70] An all-inclusive ministry, definitely.

Conclusion

Even though it is surmised that women in the Old Testament were silenced to be just wives, by reading the narratives of women in the Old Testament we gain a different picture. The Bible elevates women and records the stories of women of God in God-given positions of power and influence. From Genesis and scattered throughout the Old and New Testaments, we see women given Value, Visibility, Voice, and Vocational opportunities. © The Bible does not condone the silencing nor subjugation of women or exclude them from leadership roles.

The Church must base its practices on a thus saith the Lord, Zachariah 4:6, Joel 2:28, Galatians 3:28, 1 Corinthians 12:11 "All these are empowered by one and the same Spirit, who apportions to each one individually as he wills". There is no escaping that the Lord called women and men as He wills. God's gifts to the church are without regard to human distinctions of gender, ethnicity, nationality or hereditary. Today, we ought to ensure that our policies and practices line up with the truth about women in the Bible.

Deborah's story challenges our thinking as to a level playing field for women, be it in society or the church. Her narrative serves as a hermeneutical key to unlock the answers to the questions:

1. Does the Bible silence or forbid women to speak?

2. Does the Bible forbid women to exercise authority? The

answer to each of these questions is no.

Does the Bible give clear teaching on a theology about women? A resounding yes. Should women be allowed equal

---

[70] Review and Herald, July 5, (1895).
https://m.egwwritings.org/en/book/821.14323#14328. (Accessed July 15, 2016).

access to all leadership roles in society and the church, just as their male counterparts? Yes.

If we determine our practices in the light of the scripture and not culture, women in our society will be seen and treated differently, and the cause of God through the church would be much more advanced. Women's gifts would be celebrated and not discriminated against.

Chapter 3
Jesus and Women: Women in the New Testament

"It is by standing up for the rights of girls and women that we truly measure up as men."—*Desmond Tutu, South African cleric and theologian*

Synopsis

Jesus expressed great interest in women and children. They were often among the marginalised, the ostracised, and the victimised in his day, and they still are today. They were debarred from many opportunities because of their gender, and they received fewer wages for the same performance. They were not included in the privileges and laws of the day. Men made the deals and women were excluded; property was owned in the name of the male, only. Genealogies were reckoned by males; female names were omitted and obliterated. Only men could issue a divorce. That's just how it was. There was no suffragette movement back then, no feminists or activists, but Jesus came along amid what can be construed as a male-privileged society and proclaimed justice for women; Jesus did not fail to place a high price on women, children, and those who were considered socially marginalised because the inclusive nature of the kingdom of God ran counter to the conventions of his day.

In the kingdoms of men and the nations of this world, race, gender, ethnicity, education, age, status, and wealth determine one's participation or exclusion from many facets of life. However, this is not so in the kingdom of God. The Bible says in Romans 2:11 that God is no respecter of persons. Jesus inaugurated an apparent "Upside-down Kingdom" where we see contrasting realities: "The first shall be last, and the last first", those who try to save their life lose it, and those who lose their life for Christ's sake will find it, those who worked all day, got the same wage as those who worked one hour; prodigals are celebrated and legalist relegated; Samaritans are commended, and women appreciated. This "Upside-down Kingdom" is one of inclusivity, in which everyone has an opportunity. Jesus fought for a just Society.

The place of women in the first-century Roman world and the Jewish culture is well documented.

Firstly, "Not all women in the ancient world were on the same level. Nationally or socially, Greek women had less power than Roman women and elite women had significantly more power

84

and freedom than women of lower classes being able to initiate divorce and in certain cases own property. Jewish women had less power in one sense but in another were given a greater degree of dignity and respect in their own culture. The culture itself made it possible for traditional roles to be negotiated; in this respect it is impossible to separate the New Testament writings from the complexity of their heritage and wider context."[71]

Many Jewish women were forbidden to speak publicly to a male and were not considered credible to appear as witnesses. A witness was commonly used in everyday life. According to Jewish convention, female witnesses were on the list of persons who were not competent to testify.

> Some philosophers believed that women were capable of the same virtues as men *(Sen. Dial.* 6.16.1; Diog. Laert. 6.1.12; Crates *Ep.* 28), despite their weaker emotional constitution (Sen. *Dial.* 6.7.3). Nevertheless, moral expectations were generally lower for women, who were suspected to have a greater propensity for adultery (Diod. Sic. 1.59.3-4) and other passions (Plut. *Bride* 48, *Mor.* 145DE), evil plans (Publ. Syrus 365, 376), secretive evil (Publ. Syrus 20), divisiveness (Juv. *Sat.* 6.242-43), instability and untrustworthiness (Char. *Chaer.* 1.4.1-2), and so forth. Some writers doubted the veracity of women (Avianus *Fables* 15-16), hence their trustworthiness as witnesses in court (Justin, *hist.* 2.10.6). This broader Mediterranean distrust for women's witness appears also in Jewish tradition (Jos. *Ant.* 4.219; Sifra VDDeho. pq. 7.45.1.1)[72]

Ancient Judaism literature reflected positive and negative views of women. Josephus, a Jewish historian, points to the Law that

---

[71] David M. Scholer, "Women," in Dictionary of Jesus and the Gospels, ed. Joel B. Green, Scot McKnight, and I. Howard Marshall (Downers Grove, IL: InterVarsity, 1992), p. 22.

[72] CBE International. https://www.cbeinternational.org/resource/more-roles-women-antiquity/. (Accessed August 12, 2022).

declares "women to be inferior in all matters and should be submissive"; Philo, a Jewish philosopher, "argues that women ought to stay at home, desiring a life of seclusion"; Sirach, an Apocrypha book, states, "better is the wickedness of a man than a woman who does good; it is a woman who brings shame and disgrace." (Sir. 42:14 NRSV)[73] "The harsh statements Ben Sira makes about women reflect the kind of instruction young Jewish males were exposed to in the early second century B.C. His patriarchal perspective is as unfair as it is one-sided."[74]

"Tosefta Berakhot 6:18 teaches in the name of Rabbi Yehuda ben Ilai (mid-2nd c. CE) that every (Jewish) man is obligated to recite three blessings daily. These express gratitude for one's station in life through the negative statements: thank God that I am not a gentile, a woman, or a slave (or in earlier formulations, a boor)"[75] The Talmud (The central text of Rabbinic Judaism and the primary source of Jewish religious law (*halakha*) and Jewish theology"[76] suggested that a woman's place was in the home and that a man was not allowed to speak to a woman in public. It is against this backdrop we can better appreciate Jesus's interaction with women.

"How readest thou?"

The prophet Isaiah predicted that Messiah would come and His message of the kingdom of God would bring healing for the blind, the deaf, people with limited mobility; captives re-leased and the oppressed freed. The kingdom of God would also inaugurate a transformation at the very heart of the social and political structures, their norms and practices. "The Spirit of the Lord GOD *is* upon me; because the LORD hath anointed me to preach good tidings unto the meek; he hath sent me to bind up the broken-hearted, to proclaim liberty to the captives, and the opening of the prison to *them that are* bound." (Isaiah 61:1)

---

[73] https://bible.usccb.org/bible/sirach/25. (Accessed August 18, 2016).
[74] Ibid., https://bible.usccb.org/bible/sirach/25. (Accessed May 13, 2016).
[75] https://www.bc.edu/content/dam/files/research_ sites/cjl/texts/cjrelations/resources/sourcebook/shelo_ asani_goy.htm. (Accessed may 18, 2016).
[76] https://en.wikipedia.org/wiki/Talmud. (Accessed May 18, 2016).

The Gospel of Mark's portrait of Jesus is that of an authoritative figure, declaring the radical nature of the kingdom of God. It is a kingdom that is on the loose, launching an assault on the principalities and powers, tearing down strongholds, challenging structures and ideologies, and changing the price tags on women, children, slaves, prodigals, prostitutes, and people who were considered outcasts and of low economic output.

The Gospel of Luke portrays the fulfilment of Isaiah's prediction that the spirit of the Lord will bring a paradigm shift in society's values in Jesus's cataclysmic clash with the powers that be, and his cry against injustice as recorded in Luke 4:18, "The Spirit of the Lord *is* upon me because he hath anointed me to preach the gospel to the poor; he hath sent me to heal the broken-hearted, to preach deliverance to the captives, and recovering of sight to the blind, to set at liberty them that are bruised."

Jesus Gave Women Value.

Jesus had a hand in the creation of woman, He made her in the image and likeness of God (Themselves). Both Adam and Eve were made to reflect the oneness that exists between Jesus, the Father and the Holy Spirit. St. John confirms "For there are three that bear record in heaven, the Father, the Word, and the Holy Ghost: and these three are one." 1 John 5:7 We have already established that oneness, equality, (no hierarchy) and love, characterise the image of God. This oneness is fundamental to the nature or image of who God is and their expressed desire is that the same be replicated, not only in male-female relationships but in his followers, the body of Christ.

"Wherefore shall a man leave his father and mother and they twain shall become one flesh." No hierarchy. Mark 10:9. Jesus also prayed for his image to be reflected in relationships amongst believers, "Holy Father, keep through thine own name those whom thou hast given me, that they may be one, as we are." Yes, that his disciples would be one, even as He and the Father were one. **Rightly interpreted, Jesus's words mean, that He did not**

want any divisions, inequality or hierarchy among his followers.

I've established the above to give a preview as it were into Jesus's mindset concerning women and men. Not only did Jesus turn over the tables in the temple, but he also turned over society's conventions about how women are seen and treated. Jesus's regard for women was much different from that of his contemporaries. The following pages of this chapter are dedicated to give us a clearer insight into what God and his son Jesus taught and felt about women.

Jesus treated women with high regard throughout the Gospels. Contrary to the custom of his day, Jesus regularly addressed women in public. In the Gospel of St John chapter 4:9, we see Jesus interacting with a woman publicly, and with a woman of a race that Jews were forbidden to speak with. "Then saith the woman of Samaria unto him, how is it that thou, being a Jew, askest drink of me, which am a woman of Samaria". The Samaritan woman is surprised that Jesus should ask her for a drink, why? Because Jesus shows himself ready to disregard the customary hostile presumption regarding Samaritan women.

Jesus is the Saviour who rescues women from challenging life circumstances. He rescues the woman caught in adultery, intervened for the widow of Nain, healed the woman with the issue of blood, and blessed many others. He often frequented the home of Mary and Martha, and Mary's anointing of Jesus's feet raised many eyebrows because of her reputation as recorded in the Gospel of Luke 7:36-50. In each case where the story is mentioned in the Gospels, the woman's action is criticised.

The Gospel traditions show Jesus as not being confined to the social norms of his day regarding women. Jesus's attitude to women is made explicit in his teachings, almost without exception, women are presented in a favourable light, while the opposite tends to be the case in Rabbinic parables. Jesus's attitude to women is made clear in his interactions with them and such empirical data can only be found in the narratives about women which serve as a hermeneutical key to unlock the answers about a woman's value and roles.

Not only did Jesus speak with women but He also spoke to them in a thoughtful, caring manner. When He spoke to the woman with the bleeding disorder, **He called her "daughter."** Matthew 9:20-22. **He referred to another infirmed woman as 'the daughter of Abraham' giving women equal spiritual status as the men who called themselves the 'sons of Abraham'.** Luke 13:10-17. The New Testament is replete with examples of Jesus's attitude toward women. Jesus healed Peter's mother-in-law. Matthew 8:14-15. He met a widow who was burying her only son, and He raised that son for her. Luke 7:11-17 He went into the synagogue on the Sabbath day and in front of the religious leaders, He defended and helped a woman who was hopelessly bent over for 18 years. He spoke to her, put His hands on her and caused her to stand erect. Luke 13:10-17.

Jesus demonstrated how a man ought to value and treat a woman. Jesus said a woman is not an object of sexual gratification, to lust over, "You have heard that it was said to those of old, 'You shall not commit adultery.' But I say to you that whoever looks at a woman to lust for her has already committed adultery with her in his heart." Matthew 5:27, 28. Jesus taught that women have rights as individuals and that they were to be respected and not molested. He taught His followers to discipline their thoughts and in doing so, create an environment where men and women can work in harmony with one another, safely. Jesus defended the rights of women to be free from sexual harassment. He went as far as to say that even to think lustfully about a woman, was to commit adultery.

Jesus healed many women and cast demons out of others, displaying His care for them. Some are only briefly recorded; others are given in more detail. The message however is the same – Jesus valued women. The proliferation of stories of women and Jesus is unheard of or conceived outside of the Christian movement; they certainly speak volumes about his cry for justice for women.

Why Jesus spoke up for women?

Jesus's interest in and value for women lies at the very core of a happy home and stable society, robbing a woman of her value upsets God and society. The value of women in the plan of God is indispensable. God placed a high value on women when he created them in his image. After the fall, Jesus came via a woman to the enigma of many. Everyone born into this world owes their life to a woman. That does not sound like a curse to me. Through a woman, God chose to populate the earth. William Wallace said, "The Hand That Rocks the Cradle Is the Hand That Rules the World."[77]

Happy home, happy life, happy society, if you upset the God-given ideal for women and men in relationships, the home, church and society will pay a price. God's plan for community and unity was based on women's equal and full participation in the affairs of life.

Like that of Jesus's and Paul's time, maleness and femaleness matter in our culture. But our beliefs and practices should not be determined by the culture but by scripture. Often the kingdom of God is counterculture. In the kingdom of God, all who believe become children of God, and joint heirs, equal.

Jesus Gave Women Voice

Jesus used women frequently in His illustrations. This may not mean much to you, but it was a big thing in His day. He talked about the Queen of the South who travelled so far to find the truth. He compared the kingdom of heaven to the leaven worked into dough, made by a woman. He likened his second coming to two women working in the field. He mentioned a widow to teach a lesson about receiving God's blessings, and Jesus told a parable about a woman who lost a coin. The church, the object of his affection of which He is head, is likened to virgins, in the parable

---

[77] The Hand That Rocks the Cradle (poem). (2022, September 28). In Wikipedia. https://en.wikipedia.org/wiki/.

of the Ten Virgins. He likened his love for the church to the love of a husband for his bride. What more noble and elevated analogies could He draw on to include women who were despised in his day?

Mark 16:9 records, *"Now when Jesus was risen early the first day of the week, he appeared first to Mary Magdalene, out of whom he had cast seven devils."* There is something very remarkable in this passage of sacred history. None of the apostles, or male disciples, were honoured with the first visions of the angels, or with the immediate news of Christ's resurrection. The Saviour's first post-resurrection commission was to a woman. Not to angels, or apostles, not to the faithful Joseph, but to a woman! And not the noblest of women, i.e., his mother or Anna, but Mary, out of whom he casted seven devils!

The angel in Mark 16:7,10 said to her, "But go, tell his disciples and Peter, 'He is going ahead of you into Galilee. There you will see him, just as he told you.' "She went and told them that had been with him, as they mourned and wept. Verse 11 states: "And they, when they heard that he was alive, and had seen of her, disbelieved." Remember, according to the laws of that time, a woman was not considered among those credible to be a witness, yet we see Jesus commissioning a woman, clearly pushing back the boundaries and conventions of his day with his own "Me too" movement (on behalf of marginalised women) affirming one with a questionable background. Why would Jesus risk commissioning this incredible story to a woman who was not considered a witness and one who once had a questionable past?

Jesus spared no effort to give women back their voices. If Mary of Magdala could be given back her voice! Then all women are included. Amen! There is hope for all women in the world. What a bold and audacious move to have made 2000 years ago! Yes, Jesus restored women's voices.

Talking about voice, please permit me to use my preaching voice here.! In Jesus we see that our value is not determined by social conventions:

• None is so sunken in sin that Christ cannot redeem them.

- None has behaved so terribly to be excluded from His love.

- None is so bad as to be excluded from the purpose of His death.

- None is so bad as to be beyond the reach of His resurrection power.

- None has wandered so far that they cannot return.

Look at the extremist forms of sin. We can regard them all with the assurance that Jesus forgives tax collectors, murderers, adulterers, prostitutes, thieves, and respectable worldlings.

Jesus gave women Visibility

Jesus didn't simply give women Value and Voice to remain in obscurity, He gave women Visibility. For of Mary Magdalene, it is said, for H*e appeared first, not to John who leaned upon his breast, but to Mary Magdalene, out of whom he had cast seven devils.* Many women followed Jesus as disciples. He did not simply choose to use women as illustrations, but He was also concerned that women sit under His teachings. Women weren't allowed to do so in His day. Women sat differently from men. Today, women and men sit together and hear the teaching and preaching of the Word of God, but it just wasn't so in Jesus' time. In 1 Cor. 14:35 Paul wrote: "And if they will learn anything, let them ask their husbands at home: for it is a shame for women to speak in the church." According to the law when Paul gave this exhortation, women were not to engage in public enquiry but rather wait until they were in private to make enquiry of their husband.

Over and over in the gospels, women are given visibility: It was a woman who anointed Jesus' feet. It was a woman who anointed His head. Martha is often thought of as a woman who helped to provide meals for the church group, as though that was her ministry. Luke 8 tells us about women like Mary Magdalene, Joanna, Susanna, Mary the mother of James and Joses, and

Salome, women who followed and laboured right alongside Jesus and the disciples.

Women were the last to prepare Jesus's body with spices, and the first to see the post resurrected Christ. Jesus went against the conventions of his day to give women visibility by immortalising their stories. "Truly I tell you, wherever this gospel is preached throughout the world, what she has done will also be told, in memory of her." Matthew 26:13. Beyond doubt, the narratives of women serve as a hermeneutical key in interpreting what the Bible teaches about women.

Notice how the disciples were prejudiced against women and reflected their cultural taboos: when they recorded some of the great miracles performed by Jesus, they would exclude women. In Matthew's telling of the feeding of the five thousand, he relates that after the crowd had eaten and were satisfied, the disciples gathered up the leftover loaves and fish in baskets. The account concludes, "And those who ate were five thousand men, not counting women and children" Matt 14: 21. Mark and Luke note that five thousand men were fed Mark 6:44, Luke 9:14. Women and children are not included in the final tally. What if women and children were included in the count? How many might have been there? The disciples reflected their cultural biases against women, like some followers of Christ today.

Drawing on the work of sociologists, Megan McKenna suggests in her book "Not Counting Women and Children" (Orbis, 1994) noted "that the ratio of women and children to adult men would be 5 to 1 or 6 to 1, so the size of the crowd would be much larger. She also suggests that it is likely that women were the ones who would have taken care to pack provisions in baskets when families set out to follow Jesus. The disciples were able to produce loaves and fish because mothers thought to bring them along. Then as now, women usually plan, cook, bake, and pack the food to be eaten at a church potluck or family gathering. According to this scenario, women and children outnumbered the men, and women played a key role with Jesus in feeding the crowd. Their presence was significant, yet it is overlooked by

Mark and Luke and given only a sideways glance by Matthew."[78]

The disciples like many of the leaders of today did not think women mattered equally, St. Matthew 19:14 and St. Mark 10:14 record Jesus's rebuke to the disciples. "Suffer the little children to come unto me and forbid them not". The attitude meted out to the children also speaks to the way the women were perceived.

As we observe Jesus's interaction with women, He made a point to give them prominence and visibility. While his disciples counted women out, Jesus counted women in.

Some theologians point out that Jesus in the first instance chose twelve men to be His disciples/apostles, however, this did not mean that he intended to exclude women from being disciples. Jesus also chose twelve Jewish men for ministry.

However, this did not mean that the Gentiles (the rest of the world) would be excluded from ministry. This was not prescriptive but descriptive. David M. Scholer, in his article titled "Women," says, "More significant is the fact the Twelve did not constitute or provide the model or framework for leadership or authority in the early church, apart from the earliest days in the Jerusalem church. Rather, what was significant for the character of leadership in the early church was Jesus' call to discipleship and its definition in terms of service and the fact that both men and women were among Jesus' followers as disciples and proclaimers."[79]

In his dying moments on the cross, Jesus said to John, "Behold thy mother," John 19:26,27. In his dying moments, in excruciating pain, He remembered his mother.

When he was being crucified and the male disciples fled for their lives, the gospel records that the women were there to dress his body and we know on the glorious Sunday morning of his

---

[78] Megan McKenna "Not Counting Women and Children" (Orbis, 1994) p. 123.
[79] David M. Scholer, "Women," in Dictionary of Jesus and the Gospels, ed. Joel B. Green, Scot McKnight, and I. Howard Marshall (Downers Grove, IL: InterVarsity, 1992), 886.

resurrection, these devout women who were his disciples were his followers in death and beyond. Jesus commissioned these followers and made them Apostles by sending Mary to the disciples to tell them of his resurrection and leaving a memorial for all women. "Verily I say unto you, wheresoever this gospel shall be preached in the whole world, *there* shall also this, that this woman hath done, be told for a memorial of her." Matthew 26:13.

Jesus had female disciples

Luke 8:1-3 "And it came to pass afterward, that he went throughout every city and village, preaching and shewing the glad tidings of the kingdom of God: and **the twelve were with him,** **2** **And certain women**, which had been healed of evil spirits and infirmities, Mary called Magdalene, out of whom went seven devils, **3** **And Joanna the wife of Chuza Herod's steward, and Susanna, and many others,** which ministered unto him of their substance.

Please note, "The twelve were with him, and certain women, and Joanna...and Susanna and many others." A disciple was one who followed Christ.

We see women among the 120 persons gathered in the upper room. Acts 1:13-14 "And when they were come in, they went up into an upper room, where abode both Peter, and James, and John, and Andrew, Philip, and Thomas, Bartholomew, and Matthew, James the son of Alphaeus, and Simon Zelotes, and Judas the brother of James. **14** These all continued with one accord in prayer and supplication, **with the women, and Mary the mother of Jesus**, and with his brethren".

The Four Gospels, Matthew, Mark, Luke and John, give us a glorious opportunity to examine the paradigm shift Jesus introduced in the way women should be seen and treated.

- Jesus associated his kingdom with women: "Another parable spake he unto them; the kingdom of heaven is like unto leaven, which a woman took, and hid in three measures of meal," (Matthew 13:33).

- He likened the church to a bride a woman: "And I John saw the holy city, New Jerusalem, coming down from God out of heaven, prepared as a bride adorned for her husband." (Revelation 21:2).

- "Verily I say unto you, among them that are born of women

there hath not risen a greater than John the Baptist."
Matthew 11:11.

- Certainly, Jesus was familiar with this text from the book of
  wisdom, Solomon: "Favour is deceitful, and beauty is vain:
  but a woman that feareth the LORD, she shall be praised."
  (Proverbs 31:30).

- Jesus's vision of God's kingdom-the reign of God, or the
  Greek "Basileia", was radically inclusive. "Verily I say unto
  you, wheresoever this gospel shall be preached in the whole
  world, *there* shall also this, that this woman hath done, be
  told for a memorial of her." (Matthew 26:13).

What an affirmation of women in a society that was patriarchal!
Without doctrine or theological argument, Jesus liberated and
elevated women, he gave them Value, Visibility, and Voice.

Jesus gave agency to women, he did not exclude but included
them, from creation, the world was incomplete without them,
therefore God made woman the crowning act of his creative
works. At the centre of the incarnation/nativity is a woman, God
could have worked a miracle otherwise. The greatest miracles
after the birth of Jesus are the stories of the passion of Christ and
the resurrection of Christ and we see no males featuring, they all
deserted the Master. It was the women who returned after the
Sabbath (Saturday) before the first day of the week (Sunday) to
prepare the body of Jesus. And it was a woman the angel
commissioned to bear testimony of the risen Christ to the male
disciples. In a society where women were excluded from being
witnesses, Jesus's choice of a woman to give breaking news about
his resurrection was very radical. Jesus, beyond doubt, re-
established women's Value, Visibility, Voice, and Vocational
opportunity. Nestled in the Incarnation, Easter and Christmas
stories is the essential role of a woman.

Finally, we must respect the wishes of a person about to die,
"Verily I say unto you, wheresoever this gospel shall be preached
throughout the whole world, this also that she hath done shall be

spoken of for a memorial of her." Mark 14:9. Jesus commanded that a worldwide memorial be instituted, not for Peter, James or John the beloved disciple, but for a woman, Mary.

"How readest thou?" How could we miss Jesus's interaction, endorsement and commissioning of women? Did Jesus take back women's voices and divine authority? Absolutely not, He affirmed them.

Conclusion

C.S. Lewis said, "I believe in Christianity as I believe that the Sun has risen, not only because I see it but because by it, I see everything else." Through Jesus's interaction with women, we can better see the place and the role of women. "God, who at sundry times and in diverse manners spake in time past unto the fathers by the prophets, **2** Hath in these last days spoken unto us by his Son." Hebrews 1:1,2. If ever we were in doubt about how women ought to be treated, we can enquire, what did Jesus do?

1.   Did Jesus give women a voice or silenced them?

2.   Did Jesus commission women (the women at the well and Mary at the tomb to go tell?) or did He limit them?

3.   Given the conventions in Jesus's day where women were not permitted to speak or converse in public or be considered credible witnesses, how will you explain the instances where women went and told others that they met Jesus and that they should meet him also? "Come see a man" and "He is risen".

4.   In a patriarchal society, how could you explain Jesus's frequent and meaningful interactions and references to women in the kingdom of God?

Having considered the S*itz im Leben* of women in the time of Jesus, Jesus was an activist, a radical, a voice for justice, a

champion to right the wrongs done to women, correcting centuries of human conventions and culture that debased and limited women.

We have seen in Chapter 1 that woman was created in the image of God which means in oneness and equality as exists in the godhead. In Chapter 2 we saw this equality in creation or co-ontology accompanied by mutuality in dominion or co-dominion extended to women who were empowered by the Holy Spirit as Prophetesses and Judge in their rights. In this Chapter, 3, we examined Jesus's interaction with women and how he went beyond the conventions of his day to give women Value, Visibility, Voice, and commissioning.

The reign of God constantly challenges us to love, to forgive, to do justly, to love mercy, to be humble, to exert ourselves, to go the extra mile, to risk in order to restore, to give without hope of receiving, to stand when we feel like falling, to rise, even when we have fallen: to speak against injustice on behalf of any in the kingdom of God. The reign of God is good news: victimisation and discrimination are alleviated, nationalism and racism are eradicated, children and women are validated, men are no longer emasculated, workers are duly compensated and the addicted and fallen are reinstated. No wonder, Jesus taught us to pray "Thy kingdom come".

Jesus came preaching the good news of the kingdom of God that God reigns and rules over everything. His miracles demonstrated the power of the kingdom of God. He reached out to people who were lost, uplifted those who were downtrodden, restored health to the diseased, and forgave all manner of sin. Outcasts became insiders, tax collectors became deacons and prostitutes became proclaimers. Jesus taught us to love our enemies and to do well to them. These are some of the principles of his kingdom, as it were, an Upside-down Kingdom: In the meantime, society, the church, you and I, have a responsibility to speak to justice, to cry out against victimisation, and discrimination, to speak up against domestic violence, incest, stalking, rape, human trafficking, sex for favours, sexism, racism, nationalism, favouritism, nepotism, and misogyny. Jesus gave women Value, Visibility, Voice, and inclusion in what was seen as a male-oriented ministry.

Chapter 4
Silence and submission? Was St. Paul a misogynist?

"Feminism isn't about making women strong. Women are already strong. It's about changing the way the world perceives that strength." – G.D. Anderson

Synopsis

Stories regarding women in the Old and New Testaments confirm that women were highly valued in the Bible and were called by God to both speak and exercise authority. This was evidenced in eleven female prophets in the Bible whose main functions were to speak and to exercise authority. We've seen this in the cases of Deborah, Miriam and Phillip's four daughters, who were prophets. Jesus came along in a patriarchal society and went against the conventions of his day and gave women Value, Visibility, Voice, and Vocational opportunity.

The Apostle Paul would stand aghast to know that a letter he wrote to the church of Ephesus in AD 62 would be applied to a congregation in Johannesburg, New York, Sidney, Kingston or London in 2025, without extrapolating the *Sitz im Leben* or life setting of the text. The Apostle wrote letters to individual churches because counsels he gave to one church, i.e., in Ephesus, would not apply to the church in Colossae and vice versa. If we take his statements out of their immediate contexts and group them all, it might appear that he is saying different things at different times. Yes, and that's precisely what he did, he said different things at different times to different audiences, but he never contradicted himself. Context always determines meaning.

Therefore, if we are to be consistent and accept the inspiration of all the scriptures, the Apostle Paul could not contradict the scriptures. Paul affirmed women leaders; he appointed women to speak on his behalf and admonished them on how they should conduct themselves when speaking in public. The Apostle Paul was too familiar with the Old Testament and the influence of women who were led by the Spirit, to say otherwise. He was certainly in agreement with Joel 2:28 which prophesied that the Holy Spirit would be poured out on men and women alike.

This chapter addresses:

- **Issues related to interpreting the scriptures**
- **Harmonising the Apostle Paul's statements on women with the rest of the scriptures.**

Paul identified women with various gifts in the church. Paul was unequivocal about the status of women when he stated that the markers of society should not exist in the church "For all of you who were baptised into Christ have clothed yourselves with Christ. There is neither Jew nor Greek, there is neither bond nor free, there is neither male nor female: for ye are all one in Christ Jesus." Galatians 3:27, 28. The Apostle Paul did not have a bias against women at all, far from it, he sought to empower them, and otherwise he would have contradicted himself, other Bible authors and Jesus.

Stories regarding women in the Old and New Testaments confirm that women were highly valued in the Bible and were called by God to both speak and exercise authority. This was evidenced in eleven female prophets in the Bible whose main functions were to speak and to exercise authority. We've seen this in the cases of Deborah, Miriam and Phillip's four daughters, who were prophets. Jesus came along in a patriarchal society and went against the conventions of his day and gave women Value, Visibility, Voice, and Vocational opportunity.

Context always determines meaning.

Communication has content, context and meaning. Take any communication out of its context and it can convey an entirely different meaning. When persons are not around to give the meaning of their content (communication) and worse yet, when there is inadequate information on the context of the content, some investigation must be carried out before interpreting or even applying a person's words. (The work of exegesis and hermeneutics)

So, what did the Apostle Paul mean by those injunctions that imply that women should be silent, not teach or exercise authority? Did the Apostle Paul contradict himself and the entire scriptures, including Jesus? Absolutely not! Indeed, the Apostle Paul said what he said, and it is inspired, but the question is, what did he mean? To answer the question, we need to obtain a picture of the context that warranted the injunctions and then deduce the meaning of his words.

This chapter does just that, it explores the controversial prohibitions the Apostle Paul made that seem to favour a less than equal status for women. It harmonises these prohibitions with others of his own, which empower women and places Paul's statements alongside the rest of the scriptures, which by their very nature, are a coherent whole.

Principles of interpretation

We hold dear to this principle that all the scriptures are inspired; however, all the scriptures cannot be applied arbitrarily. No pericope or text or passage of the scriptures stands independently of the rest of the scriptures. If all the scriptures are given by the inspiration of God (from the same source), therefore, no singular passage of the scriptures would contradict another. The Bible is God's inspired word to man and not man's words about God. We have a double obligation to rightly interpret what God says because how we use the Bible will impact people's view of God. Therefore, no part of the Bible is of private interpretation, each part must harmonise with the whole. Isolated passages of the Bible cannot be used to justify the discrimination against males or females who were created in the image and likeness of God, possessing his characteristics of unity and equality.

Jesus quoted the Old Testament and agreed with it. The New Testament writers quoted the Old Testament frequently and agreed with the prophets in the Old Testament. Since all the scriptures are given by inspiration, would Paul single-handedly contradict the witness of the Old Testament and Jesus on women? Absolutely not. We ought to protect the unity and integrity of the scriptures; therefore, when in doubt about a particular passage, we have the rest of the inspired writings to throw light on difficult or controversial passages; line-up-line; precept on precept, and when it gets even more difficult, we must apply Paul's injunction to "Study to show ourselves approved unto God...rightly dividing the word of truth". This is doing the work of exegesis and hermeneutics.

An important hermeneutical question to be considered when interpreting the scriptures is, is the pericope or passage an endorsement? All scriptures were inspired by God but not all scripture is an endorsement or exhortation to be executed. There are examples in the Old Testament of abuse and murder; these are certainly not endorsements.

Another hermeneutical question is whether the scripture is prescriptive or descriptive. The way women were treated in the time of Jesus, was that prescriptive or descriptive? Was the male priesthood of the Old Testament and the twelve Jewish male disciples intended to be prescriptive or descriptive; were all future disciples to be male and probably Jewish also? Absolutely not. St. Paul instructed slave owners on how to treat slaves. Does this imply that Paul was prescribing slavery? Was he saying that slavery is, okay? Certainly not.

In the recording of the feeding of the 5,000, Matthew, Mark and Luke all reported this occasion and said, "Not counting women and children." Is that prescriptive? Should women and children be excluded when recording important historical events or happenings in the life of the church or society? Certainly not. The Bible says that the scriptures were written for our examples. This is interesting because you can have examples of what to do and examples of what not to do, examples of how to do things and examples of how not to do things. Determining the difference is the work of hermeneutics.

When attempting to get the meaning of a problematic pericope or passage of the scriptures, begin by establishing what is already evident on the subject and use it to interpret the unclear or obscure, not the other way around. Finally, on interpretation, a good hermeneutical question is, what did Jesus do?

The Apostle Paul encouraged the young Timothy to "Study to show himself approved." 2 Timothy 2:15, he was referring to the study of the Old Testament scriptures; the New Testament was not yet formed. He continued, "Rightly dividing the word of truth". That exhortation is also an injunction to the church and custodians of the scriptures today to "Rightly divide the word of truth". Rightly dividing the word of truth for us would mean applying the disciplines of exegesis and hermeneutics. These disciplines help us to have at least a small appreciation for the text written in its context 2,000 years ago, of which we know little.

What is exegesis?

Exegesis lays bare the historical sense of the text. It puts limits on what a text says and does not say. Rightly done, it employs the tools of word studies, syntax, grammar, and historical and literary criticism, as lenses through which we can see the text. The wisdom and value of the scriptures can only be valid with proper exegesis or when considered in their S*itz im Leben*, or life setting.

What is Hermeneutics? Hermeneutics is the process of naming the contemporary sense and significance of the text and its implications for an audience. When we search for the meaning in a text, we allow the text to serve its God-intended function. The goal of hermeneutics is not only what was meant in history, but today; therefore, deconstruction is essential to this task. To find the meaning of the text, literary and higher criticism are essential, as also theological criticism, which asks and answers questions about what God is doing in and behind the text and whether the meaning harmonises with other teachings about God.

The Scribes and Pharisees were very good at quoting the scriptures, they often interrogated Jesus, thinking that they could trap him, but Jesus would confidently explain to them the true meaning of his own words. Jesus framed what I call a hermeneutical question, "How readest thou?" Luke 10:26. By inference, he meant, do you understand the meaning of what you've read? What do the words mean?

Understanding Bible Genre

Quoting and applying the scriptures should be done within context, content and meaning. In the first instance, one must understand the nature of the text or pericope before them; what genre it is. The scriptures comprise various genres; the Old Testament, for example, is comprised of Law, History, Prophecy, Poetry, and Psalms, etc. The New Testament: Parables, History, Prophecy, Poetry, Epistles and Letters of Occasion, all inspired, however, Letters of Occasion or Epistles were often written to address situations in a particular historical context.

As an itinerant pastor who developed many churches, the

Apostle Paul would often be contacted by letter from the local church leaders; in return, he would respond by letter to them, giving specific advice to issues raised in their letters or sending greetings and exhortations. What the Apostle Paul said to the Ephesians would not have applied to the Romans or Corinthians and vice versa; hence he wrote different letters, (Letters of Occasion) all inspired but not all applicable to other churches in Asia Minor.

If all the scriptures were universally applicable, the Apostle Paul would have written one letter and circulated it across the board, rather than writing several letters to different churches. However, each church had its independent situations and issues; hence letters were commissioned and addressed to the church in Ephesus, Sardis, Philadelphia etc. It is not one size fits all. I think that's what we do today; we just take these personal letters and apply them universally. Yes, the scriptures are inspired and were written for our examples, but we cannot just apply them arbitrarily.

Deciding on the meaning of a particular scripture is not always a simple exercise, especially when dealing with passages that appear to be controversial or contradicting something taught elsewhere in the scriptures. A couple of examples are the smoking guns the Church uses to perpetuate a theology that limits women, namely, St. Paul's exhortations, "Let your women keep silence in the churches: for it is not permitted unto them to speak; but they are commanded to be under obedience as also saith the law. And if they will learn anything, let them ask their husbands at home: for it is a shame for women to speak in the church." 1 Corinthians 14:34-35. Also, 1 Timothy 2:12 KJV: "But I suffer not a woman to teach, nor to usurp authority over the man, but to be in silence."

Really! Are all women to remain silent in all churches? Let us just take a closer look at the literal words of these texts and apply them, and we will do the exegesis later in the chapter. Indeed, the church does not apply these texts today and never did. We do not have a policy that women should not speak in churches. Women have been at the forefront of teaching, exhorting, praying, and prophesying in many churches and educational institutions.

When we find apparent anomalies or contradictions in the scriptures, we must pull out all the exegetical and hermeneutical tools: concordances, dictionaries, commentaries and narratives about women, etc. We must engage in Bible study, not as tourists or browsers: hurriedly observing what appears to be on the surface, but rather, we would study as an explorer, stopping by and paying attention to details, taking pictures from different angles, reading up the history and indeed if necessary, digging for details.

The harmony of Apostle Paul and other Bible narratives. The stories of women in the Bible are like parables; they contain hidden messages that the hurried reader would not observe. The Bible says that Jesus taught not without a parable; many of the teachings and wisdom of the scriptures lie not in the surface reading of the text but in the text, and behind the text. Narratives of women, when put together, serve as a hermeneutical key to unlocking the meaning of some of the most complex and controversial scripture passages about women, because they contain nuggets of truth in a non-confrontational and indirect way.

What the Bible teaches about women is not always discernible by the traditional proof-text approach of line upon line or precept upon precept, or what I refer to as the concordance approach (that's pretty easy), to the contrary, toward a theology about women is irrefutably embedded and substantiated in the stories and narratives of women in the Bible.

Introducing and managing change may require strategies that enable transition without much confrontation, hence, Jesus often spoke in parables or stories. We can even take this to another level by saying the narratives about women serve not only as a hermeneutical tool but also make good comedy. Like in the case of Sisera the man, who fled before Deborah, a woman. Where were the strong and courageous males when Jesus needed them most in the Garden of Gethsemane, Good Friday on the eve of the crucifixion and Easter Sunday morning? Could it be that these details surrounding the story of Jesus's death and resurrection with the females alone showing up, juxtaposed with the ascribed status of the men being the head and the leaders but were nowhere to be found, for fear or discouragement, is scandalous? Isn't that ironic that the women who were not to be seen or considered witnesses became the heroines in the story? Do the details in this story contain satire or sarcasm hidden from surface readers? Do true leaders walk away or are they present?

Does this story invite its listeners to conclude that true leadership has nothing to do with gender, but with responsibility? Like the answer to the question who is your neighbour? The story of The Good Samaritan redefines neighbour, not in terms of proximity, geography, or cultural sensitivity but in terms of need. Could it be that in the details of the story surrounding Jesus's pre-resurrection, we see that leadership has nothing to do with gender but rather the exercise of courage in the face of personal threat and loss of hope? Can we read the same in the story of David, the shepherd boy who became a hero because he took a stand and dared to challenge Goliath? Probably some stereotypes that we have been conditioned to accept as true, have little to do with what truth really is. God is not into human conventions; He is above them.

St. Paul and Women leaders

The Apostle's injunctions of silence and submission were addressed to specific audiences and were not intended to be general or universal injunctions. St. Paul himself commended women for speaking in the churches; look at some examples: "I commend to you our sister Phoebe, a deacon of the church in Cenchreae." Romans 16:1

"The churches of Asia salute you. Aquila and Priscilla salute you much in the Lord, with the church that is in their house." 1 Corinthians 16:19.

"And he began to speak boldly in the synagogue: when Aquila and **Priscilla** had heard, **they took him unto them, and expounded unto him the way of God more perfectly.**" Acts 18:26.

"Greet Prisca and Aquila, **my co-workers in Christ Jesus**, 4 who risked their necks for my life, to whom not only I give thanks but also all the churches of the Gentiles." Romans 16: 3,4.

"Greet Andronicus and Junia, my fellow Israelites who were in prison with me; they are **prominent among the apostles**, and they were in Christ before I was" Romans 16:7.

"I urge Euodia, and I urge Syntyche to be of the same mind in the Lord. 3 Yes, and I ask you also, my loyal companion, **help these women, for they have struggled beside me in the work of the gospel, together with Clement and the rest of my co-workers**, whose names are in the book of life", Philippians 4:2,3.

St. Paul personally embraced and endorsed women in ministry, his voice and actions spoke against excluding women. As a student of the Old Testament, he was thoroughly acquainted with the roles women played as prophets, judges, queens, etc. He was fully aware of Joel's prophecy that God would pour out his spirit upon all flesh, including women and maidens. (Joel 2:28) *"And it shall come to pass afterwards, that I will pour out my spirit upon all flesh; and your sons and your daughters shall prophesy, your old men shall dream dreams, your young men shall see visions: 29 And also upon the servants and upon the handmaids in those days will I pour out my spirit."*

St. Paul further outlined spiritual gifts for the church without regard to gender in 1st Corinthians 12:1-13.

> *1" Now concerning spiritual gifts, brethren, I would not have you ignorant.*
>
> *2 Ye know that ye were Gentiles, carried away unto these dumb idols, even as ye were led.*
>
> *4 Now there are diversities of gifts, but the same Spirit.*
>
> *5 And there are differences of administrations, but the same Lord.*
>
> *6 And there are diversities of operations, but it is the*

same God which worketh all in all.

7 But the manifestation of the Spirit is given to every man to profit withal.

8 For to one is given by the Spirit the word of wisdom; to another the word of knowledge by the same Spirit;

9 To another faith by the same Spirit; to another the gifts of healing by the same Spirit;

10 To another the working of miracles; to another prophecy; to another discerning of spirits; to another divers kind of tongues; to another the interpretation of tongues:

11 But all these worketh that one and the selfsame Spirit, dividing to every man severally as he will.

12 For as the body is one, and hath many members, and all the members of that one body, being many, are one body: so also is Christ.

13 For by one Spirit are we all baptised into one body, whether we be Jews or Gentiles, whether we be bond or free; and have been all made to drink into one Spirit.

The Apostle Paul was abundantly clear in establishing the nature and function of the church. All who are called into that body are given spiritual gifts not based on class, race, gender, ethnicity, or any of the like. Paul makes it very clear that the Holy Spirit gives a diversity of gifts to its members, a gender-neutral distribution of spiritual gifts if you will. God, not society, culture, or the church determines one's giftedness, abilities and calling. God can even empower a donkey, if need be, Numbers 22:31-39, why not a woman? Remember, "It's not by might nor by power but by his spirit, saith the Lord." Zechariah 4:6.

In his book, "The Key To Your Child's Heart", Gary Smalley said there are three levels of communication: content, meaning, and feeling. In hermeneutics, we consider the context, content, meaning, and application of a text. For example, a man's wife would have typically called him "honey" or "sweetheart", but when she called him by his first name, Michael! (Content) at 5:30 pm, and he should have been at home at 5:00 pm, he knows that Michael! At 5:30 pm is not simply, hello Michael, rather, in this context, Michael could mean, where are you? Are you late again? Do I have to go to the grocery store alone? Why are you treating others or your work as more important than me? Can you see what's happening behind the scenes? What is said (content) and when (context) can determine the actual (meaning).

If we consider that reading the Bible, especially the New Testament is taking the words that others said nearly 2,000 years ago, a period that we know little about the customs, idioms and the meaning of the words used, we would be very cautious in quoting any scripture which seems to be unclear.

For example, the phrase "their worm will burn forever and ever" in Mark 9:48 is an idiomatic expression; today's equivalent would be, "that advert went on forever," or "the sermon, or prayer went on forever", or "I was stuck in traffic forever", meaning, it was very long.

Another example of the danger of taking the content of a text literally without regard to the context or other references is, "And they shall go forth, and look upon the carcasses of the men that have transgressed against me: for their worm shall not die, neither shall their fire be quenched; and they shall be an abhorring unto all flesh." Isaiah 66:24. The Hebrew word "Gehenna" the place where the dead were burnt, became associated as the place of eternal fire because bodies were burnt there continually. A theology of eternal torment was later developed, based upon a surface reading of this text, but where will Gehenna be forever burning when God will create a new heaven and a new earth, and all the former things will pass away? *"And God shall wipe away all tears from their eyes; and there shall be no more death, neither sorrow, nor crying, neither shall there be any more pain: for the former things are passed away."* Revelation 21:3

Therefore, the phrase "burn forever" could not mean a perpetual fire literally because this is a blatant contradiction to other passages of scripture which state the very opposite. It does not fit with the rest of the scriptures on the teaching of life after death, nor reflect the justice and mercy of God's character. It is an idiomatic expression, meaning that the hearers understood the application in the context in which it was used.

Another hermeneutical principle is paying attention to the immediate context of a passage or text. For example, Revelation 7:4-9 which speaks about the 144000:

> "And I heard the number of them which were sealed: *and there were* sealed an hundred *and* forty *and* four thousand of all the tribes of the children of Israel.
>
> **5** Of the tribe of Juda *were* sealed twelve thousand. Of the tribe of Reuben *were* sealed twelve thousand. Of the tribe of Gad *were* sealed twelve thousand. **6** Of the tribe of Aser *were* sealed twelve thousand. Of the tribe of Nepthalim *were* sealed twelve thousand. Of the tribe of Manasses *were* sealed twelve thousand. **7** Of the tribe of Simeon *were* sealed twelve thousand. Of the tribe of Levi *were* sealed twelve thousand. Of the tribe of Issachar *were* sealed twelve thousand. **8** Of the tribe of Zabulon *were* sealed at twelve thousand. Of the tribe of Joseph *were* sealed twelve thousand. Of the tribe of Benjamin *were* sealed twelve thousand. Verses 4-8 are a detailed breakdown of 144000 people and verse nine continues, **9** After this I beheld, and, lo, a great multitude, which no man could number, of all nations, and kindreds, and people, and tongues, stood before the throne, and before the Lamb, clothed with white robes, and palms in their hands;"

The 144000 was never intended to be the total of those being saved, the very context says, "After this I beheld, and, lo, a great multitude, which no man could number". Paying attention to content and context is essential before extrapolation and application.

Doing the work of exegesis is the equivalent of what detectives do at a crime scene; cordoning off a wide area to examine every bit of evidence or implement found, meticulously examining the entire area to detect any substance, foot or fingerprint, etc. The work of exegesis involves getting into the context, the words spoken in other references, cultural nuances, and their meaning in secular culture to truly appreciate what happened and what was the occasion for the admonishment or counsel. If we fail to study well, we could fall short of understanding what the scripture(s) mean.

Other hermeneutical issues when interpreting the scriptures are syntax and punctuation. Are you aware that when the Bible was initially written they did not use punctuation, these were added after? Could you imagine the challenges that translators had to give us our versions when the originals were without commas and full stops etc.?

To illustrate the importance of punctuation let me share an illustration I heard many years ago. A manager sent his employee overseas to do some purchasing for the company, the employee informed his manager of the price of the goods. The manager responded by text saying, "No price too high". The employee in good faith purchased the stock. To the manager's surprise, an invoice landed on his desk for thousands of dollars before the employee returned. The manager quickly phoned his employee and queried why he purchased the goods at such a high price. The employee responded by saying, I responded to your text message which said, "No price too high". What the manager really meant was "No, price {is}too high". The presence of the comma conveys a different meaning. Without the comma, the saying could mean, go ahead and purchase, no price is too high. With the comma, no, "price too high" the statement means, no, do not purchase, the price is too high.

Similarly, the issue of punctuation applies to Jesus's words to the thief on the cross, "I say unto you today thou shall be with me in paradise" If we were to place a comma (,) after the word you, the text would read, "I say unto you, today thou shall be with me in

Paradise''. This would mean that both Jesus and the thief went to Paradise that day. This of course, did not happen. Jesus did not go to Paradise that day (see John 20:17); instead, He went into the tomb of Joseph of Arimathea for 3 days and was later resurrected. However, if you place the comma after the word today, the text will read, "I say on to you today, thou shalt be with me in paradise". This gives a different meaning. The text was a promise that Jesus made to the dying thief on the day of his death, that sometime in the future, meaning, on this day, I am saying to you "Thou shall be with me in Paradise".

To interpret one's words does require in-depth analysis and observation. Only when the detective work of exegesis, exploration of evidence through Bible commentaries, concordances, Lexicons and inquiry into the S*itz im Leben* can the work of hermeneutics, discovering the actual meaning behind the content, be reliable. Against this backdrop let's delve into St. Paul's statements.

Harmonising Paul's Controversial Injunctions

Three scriptural injunctions about women written by St. Paul, 1 Corinthians 11:1-4, 1 Corinthians 14:26-39, and 1 Timothy 2:11-12 have been used to subjugate women in society as a whole, create division in many churches, and led to abuse in relationships between women and men. They have been foundational in hindering women from receiving full ecclesiastical authority. Without getting into all the particulars, I want to bring the readers' attention to the genre and *Sitz im Leben* of these three injunctions.

Paul's epistles to the churches were "Letters of Occasion" wherein he addressed problems of divisiveness and discipline that were brought to his attention as well as spiritual and theological questions and concerns of some believers. As an itinerant evangelist, Paul was not stationed in one district, as some clergy are today. He wrote letters to the churches as he travelled around and as the need arose. 1 Corinthians was one such letter, to the church community in Corinth.

1 Timothy is a pastoral letter Paul wrote to Timothy who presided over the Ephesian church. Paul's letters were not general epistles but rather to a church community or to a single person. The challenge is to determine exegetically and contextually what is to be left as local and what can be applied universally.

1 Corinthians 11:1-14 addresses appropriateness in worship, mainly head covering while praying and prophesying in public, (a contradiction if women were to be silent in the churches). This pericope is not about subordination but about honouring one's source; honouring is submitting but not a rule of subordination. A woman's head covering is her hair and a man without a head covering has a shaven head; else, they were considered prostitutes.

1 Corinthians 14:26-39 addresses orderly worship. There are two instances of not speaking during worship that Paul stipulates. The first instance involves speaking in an unknown tongue: no more than three should speak, one at a time, and if there is no interpreter, the speaker is to keep quiet. 27. Then the Apostle also forbids men to speak, "If any man speaks in an unknown tongue, let it be by two, or at the most by three, and that by course; and let one interpret, but if there be no interpreter, let him keep silence in the church; and let him speak to himself, and to God". Verse 28 clearly says, "Let him keep silent in the church". A plain literal reading of the text also forbids men to speak.

Both males and females are forbidden to speak in the same pericope, but the context is very important to understand here.

The second instance has to do with women remaining silent in the churches during public worship "as the Law says" verses 33b-35. It is bad enough that scholars have portrayed Paul as contradictory from one letter to another, but will he do so in the same letter? 1 Timothy 2:11-12: "A woman should learn in quietness and full submission" seems to be a follow-up from his first injunction in Corinthians for women to learn in silence. "I do not permit a woman to teach or to have authority over a man; she must be silent." Some interpret this passage to mean that women should never teach in the assembled church; but in Chapter 11, Paul did not silence women regarding praying and prophesying during public worship.

Paul's stipulation is "as the Law says." If the women are to keep silent, and men are to keep silent, how could they have worship? Imagine a service on Zoom or Google Meet, and all microphones are muted; what kind of worship service would that be? Again, context is important.

It was lawful for men in public assemblies to ask questions or even interrupt the speaker when there was any matter in his speech that they did not understand, but this liberty was not granted to women. Roman law prohibited a woman from attempting anything in public or private that was considered a man's assignment. "In our laws, the condition of women is, in many respects, worse than that of men. Women are precluded from all public offices; therefore, they cannot be judges, nor execute the function of magistrates; they cannot sue, plead, nor act in any case, as proxies."[80]

This is so important as we begin to extrapolate not just what St. Paul said on the surface but what he meant, bearing in mind also the circumstances, the _Sitz im Leben_ of St. Paul's word is very critical. The newly formed Christian church was making great inroads into society and was already seen as a runaway group. Paul wanted to protect the integrity of the Christians by reminding them to keep Roman law which forbade women to speak in public or to be a witness. Hence the phrase "According to the law", is Roman law, not the Bible.

Compare Acts 10:28. "And he said unto them, ye know how that it is an unlawful thing for a man that is a Jew to keep company or come unto one of another nation, but God hath showed me that I should not call any man common or unclean". "An unlawful thing." Yes, Jewish law prohibited Jews from keeping company with non-Jews, just as Roman

---

[80] Adam Clarke, Commentary on the Bible, (1831). https://biblehub.com/commentaries/clarke/1_timothy/1. htm. (Accessed September 29, 2022).

law forbade women to speak in public. These were local situations that Paul was addressing.

Against this backdrop, we can appreciate Paul's stern injunction to "Let your women keep silence in the churches: for it is not permitted unto them to speak; but they are commanded to be under obedience as also saith the law". The women in Ephesus were to avoid bringing disrepute in any way to the church by disobeying "The Law." "And if they learn anything, let them ask their husbands at home: for it is a shame for women to speak in the church." Paul simply uses Roman law for women, which forbade them to speak publicly. Again, he concludes his treaty in verse 40 of chapter 14 by stating, "Let all things be done decently and in order," lawfully. Paul's concern is not silence as submission, but silence as in respect for the law. Paul was very likely prohibiting the Ephesian women, not all women, from teaching.

It may be added here that on this subject, "The Jews were very strenuous, and their laws were very strict. The Rabbis taught that a woman should know nothing but the use of the distaff, and they were specially prohibited from asking questions in the synagogue, or even from reading. The same rule is still observed by other religious groups." [81]

"It was the exclusive privilege of the men to put questions in the assembly. —ἐν ἐκκλησίᾳ) *in the assembly* either civil or sacred. —λαλεῖν, *to speak*) either in teaching or asking."[82]

It has taken centuries of agitation and protests for women to be able to vote, we now have the benefits of the suffragette movement and the feminist movement and yet we struggle to empower women. "Suffragettes' tactics were to cause disruption and some civil disobedience, such as the 'rush' on Parliament in

[81] https://www.bibliaplus.org/en/commentaries/4/al-bert-barnes-bible-commentary/1-corinthians/14/35. (Accessed 29 September, 2022).
[82] https://biblehub.com/commentaries/1_corinthians/14-35.htm. (Accessed 25 September, 2022).

October 1908 when it encouraged the public to join them in an attempt to invade the House of Commons. 60,000 people gathered but the police cordon held fast. The lack of Government action led the WSPU to undertake more violent acts, including attacks on property and law-breaking, which resulted in imprisonment and hunger strikes. These tactics attracted a great deal of attention to the campaign for votes for women."[83]

Imagine going back 2000 years ago amid a patriarchal society when Paul confronted biases against women without a suffragette movement. Imagine his strength of conviction to state unequivocally that in Christ, there is neither Jew, Gentile, male or female; that women should be put on the same strata with men in a society whose conventions grossly demeaned women. Paul was unequivocal when it came to recognising God's calling to the fairer sex.

---

[83] https://www.parliament.uk/about/living-heritage/transformingsociety/electionsvoting/womenvote/overview/startsuffragette-/. (Accessed 27th July, 2022).

Conclusion

While holding to the inspired nature of the Bible, we cannot deny that its backdrop as a patriarchal society influenced its interpretation. Patriarchal refers to a culture of male privilege, where male authority is seen as normative.

"The Hebrew and Christian scriptures originated in a patriarchal society and perpetuated the androcentric (male-centred) traditions of their culture."[84] However, Jacqueline Lapsley, said that we do not have to reject scripture as some feminists have done to condemn patriarchy. "Theological convictions need not prevent one from naming patriarchy in the text, or from telling the truth about texts that damage women; on the contrary, feminist theological convictions require these."[85]

Through reading the narratives about women we see a consistent thread in the Old and New Testaments of the Holy Spirit equipping women both to speak and exercise authority. Consequently, because of the unbiased indwelling of the Holy Spirit, women were involved in all ministry positions and activities, including judges, apostles, prophetic speaking, serving as ministers, leaders, elders, teachers, and co-workers.

The Bible teaches that spiritual authority which comes from God was given to women. There were ten righteous women called as prophets. God did not forbid women to exercise authority. Paul spoke emphatically about women in leadership, gender was not an issue and women were already involved in the church. Paul even exhorts them not to abandon their veil when they prayed or prophesied.

Was the Apostle Paul a misogynist? Certainly not; he fought for the rights and freedoms that women should have. He

---

[84] https://ms.fortresspress.com/downloads/9780800698072Chapter1.pdf. (Accessed October 10, 2022).
[85] Jacqueline E. Lapsley, Whispering the Word: Hearing Women's Stories in the Old Testament (Louisville: Westminster John Knox, 2005), p. 2.

recommended and empowered women as Jesus did; he gave women Value, Visibility, Voice, and Vocational opportunity.

St. Paul faced a multicultural society like ours today, he had to handle diversity in the face of patriarchy, yet he was unequivocal about the equality and standing of a woman in the eyes of God and the newly formed Christian Church. His theological basis for this was that the Holy Spirit calls and gifts women and men for his purposes. He also understood that Christ had to tear down the middle wall of partition that existed in society; between slaves and owners, between Jew and Gentile, and between male and female and that all who were baptised were baptised into the body of Christ to be part of the priesthood of all believers. He saw Joel 2:28, the outpouring of the Holy Spirit on maidens and women as already being fulfilled in the Old Testament and in the time of Jesus and Pentecost. Galatians 3:28 remains the icon of gender inclusiveness in the writings of Saint Paul. Instead of silencing women or taking away women's voices, St. Paul empowered them. His statements on silence were counsels of occasion. In other words, they were only applicable to the context and audience he addressed.

Does the Bible teach that women should be silenced or muted? No. In the case of women being silent, we have answered the following questions: are there examples in the Bible of women speaking? Yes. Are there examples in the Bible of women prophesying, praying, exhorting?

leading, and teaching? Yes. Did the Old Testament, New Testament or Jesus, empower women to speak? Yes. Does the Bible teach that the Holy Spirit gives gifts to men and women? Yes, (And it shall come to pass afterwards, that I will pour out my spirit upon all flesh; and your sons and your daughters shall prophesy, your old men shall dream dreams, your young men shall see visions:) Joel 2:28. 1 Cor. 12:11. The answer to each question is a resounding yes.

Therefore, when we find sparse references that seem to say otherwise, we can only conclude that its context must have been local, and then such must be exegeted and applied accordingly. It is an oxymoron to assert that women should not teach or lead because they are female when there are biblical examples to the contrary. Looking at the stories of women in the Bible attest that women both spoke and exercised authority without limitation.

In society, women speak and exercise authority: from presidents, vice presidents and prime ministers, to headmistresses in public schools and various government and private sector departments. We find a consistent pattern of women being called and gifted by God to speak and lead throughout history and in modern times. As recorded in the front pages of this book, over 130 of those named women are presidents, prime ministers or leaders in society and religious organisations. In many churches, women speak and head various ministries and departments; they wield authority. The same applies in society. In the home, women speak and exercise authority as females, whether married or unmarried, single mothers or simply single.

God made males and females in their image and likeness, reflecting God's love, oneness, unity, and equality. Jesus died to redeem both males and females and commissioned them through the power of the Holy Spirit. St. Paul was on board in his understanding that the distribution of spiritual gifts was without regard to gender and that a greater manifestation of the Holy Spirit was prophesied for the last days to be realised. The Bible does not uphold a single gender or single nationality as having pre-eminence over another.

Was the Apostle Paul a misogynist? Absolutely not, probably in today's terms a feminist, for he emphatically defended the equality of women when he stated, *"There is neither Jew nor Greek, slave nor free, male nor female, for you are all one in Christ Jesus."* Galatians 3:28. Given the *Sitz im Leben*, this was a radical statement. Paul writes, **"Therefore, my brethren...I beseech Euodias, and beseech Syntyche, that they be of the same mind in the Lord. And I entreat thee also, true yoke-fellow, help those women which labored with me in the gospel, with Clement also, and with other my fellow-laborers, whose names are in the book of life." Philippians 4:1-3. Certainly, this is a glowing affirmation of women who worked with Paul, not in tent making but in the ministry.**

Paul emphatically gave women Value, Visibility, and Voice. The Church, the custodians of God's word, has an obligation to rightly interpret the word of truth. Paul's exhortation is to end the cry of discrimination against women and create a level playing field in the home, the body of Christ and society. The scripture's mandate is for a just society for all.

"TIS one thing now to read the Bible through,

Another thing to read, to learn and do;

'Tis one thing now to read it with delight,

And quite another thing to read it right.

Some read it with design to learn to read, But

to the subject pay but little heed; Some read it

as their duty once a week, But no instruction

from the Bible seek;

Some read to prove a pre-adopted creed, Thus,

understand but little what they read; And every

passage in the Book they bend To make it suit

that all-important end."

(Autobiography of a Pioneer: Or, The Nativity, Experience, Travels, and ...By Samuel Pickard)

Chapter 5
Ordination: Gendered Privileges and Gendered Spaces!

"Women are responsible for two-thirds of the work done worldwide yet earn only 10 per cent of the total income and own 1 per cent of the property. So, are we equals? Until the answer is yes, we must never stop asking."—*Daniel Craig, British actor.*

Synopsis

Within the Christian Church, there is an impasse on the appropriate roles of women within the church. Interpretations of Pauline injunctions in 1 Timothy 2:9-15 and 1 Corinthians 14:33-38 vary. Reading the same passages of the Scriptures, some conclude that the injunctions forbidding women to speak and exercise authority are normative-universally binding for all times. Others believe that those injunctions are historically limited to time and place. Whichever perspective one takes has theological, ethical and liturgical implications for the way women are perceived and how a church conducts its ministry.

There is no issue of gender differentiation when it comes to the distribution of spiritual gifts, according to the prophets Joel and Paul, "And it shall come to pass afterwards, that I will pour out my spirit upon all flesh; and your sons and your daughters shall prophesy, your old men shall dream dreams, your young men shall see visions: And also upon the servants and upon the handmaids in those days will I pour out my spirit. (Joel 2:28, 29) God pours out his Spirit on males and females alike, isn't that clear enough? The Apostle Paul likewise asserted, "There is neither Jew nor Greek, there is neither bond nor free, there is neither male nor female: for ye are all one in Christ Jesus". (Galatians 3;28).

This view argues that although the notion of a restricted role for women in the church is predicated on an interpretation of a few verses from scripture, the overwhelming weight of scripture, favours an entirely different perspective on the issue. The Bible both implicitly and explicitly affirms the role of women in the plan of God. It does not limit the capabilities of one sex over the other as we have been taught and made to believe. The notion that there is an ontological difference regarding women either at creation or after the fall, necessitating a relationship of subordination and restriction is biblically and theologically unsound.

Does the Bible endorse women speaking and giving witness to

the gospel? Did women in the Bible teach, lead or exercise authority?

The creation account and narratives about women in the scriptures provide answers to the questions as to whether a woman should speak and exercise authority. The stories of ten righteous female prophets in the Bible confirm that God called women to lead and exercise authority. Jesus's affirmation, elevation and interactions with women confirmed the same. He intentionally gave women Value, Visibility, and Voice; He chose them as his witnesses in a culture where women were not considered credible. The Apostle Paul similarly affirmed and appointed women and referred to them as fellow labourers in ministry. The Bible confirms that women, created in God's image have been called or ordained by God to both speak and exercise authority and that the body of believers upon recognising such, give their acknowledgement by means of laying on of hands or vote.

Suppose we determine our practices in the light of Holy Scripture and not culture? In that case, we will see embedded in the stories about women in the Bible, the answers to the questions about women's nature and roles, including ones with authority. A woman's gifts from the Holy Spirit make room for her ministry. Ten female prophets including Deborah's story as a prophet and judge in the Old Testament, are sufficient to inform our thinking as to the role of women as leaders in society and the church. Jesus, through whom the Godhead manifested themselves, turned men's conventions upside down and taking a radical stance on women's behalf. The Church must follow its leader; Jesus. Women should be allowed to participate in life equally.

The Church's rationale for a theology of ordination

Whatever name the church chooses to give the service for recognising the calling of the Holy Spirit in the lives of believers; be it ordination, commissioning or laying on of hands, it should be the same for men and women. Ordination is ordination, whether of a deacon, elder or minister, whether male or female. Ordination means "to set in order & to arrange: to appoint. To set apart for a sacred office." Persons may be ordained to differing ministries, still, the act of ordaining remains the same in meaning, to set apart or appoint. For example, graduation means the successful completion of a course of study. We do not call a graduation service for males by a different name than a graduation service for females. There should only be one name for the service that recognises males and females called to minister in their area of giftedness; to do otherwise is in the least to be inconsistent, and at worst, discriminatory.

Churches must not fail to do justice; they must ensure that women's Value, Visibility, Voice, and Vocational opportunities are equally protected at all levels. The position some denominations have taken not to ordain females, or to ordain female deacons or elders but not female ministers is a contradiction and renders such practice grossly unconscionable. (He has shown you, O man, what is good. And what does the LORD require of you but to act justly, to love mercy, and to walk humbly with your God?) Micah 6:8.

In this chapter, we address the controversial subject of the full representation, participation and endorsement of women in the church, namely, ordination.

The Old Testament cites the ordination of Jeremiah, "Then the word of the Lord came unto me, saying, Before *I formed thee* in the belly *I knew thee*, and before thou camest forth out of the womb *I sanctified thee*, and *I ordained thee* a prophet unto the nations." Jeremiah 1:5.

God, the Holy Spirit, is the one who does the ordaining or setting aside, not a creed or a committee but the sovereign will and foreknowledge of God who predestines whomsoever they will.

Jesus said to his disciples **"You did not choose Me, but I chose you and appointed you that you should go and bear fruit".**

(John 15:16)

St. Paul said, "Take heed therefore unto yourselves, and to all the flock, over thee which the Holy Ghost hath made you overseers" (*Acts 20:28*).

It is the Holy Ghost that calls and sets persons apart for spiritual things. Another example of one's calling is found in the book of Acts chapter 9, verses 10-15 where the Holy Spirit spoke to Ananias in a dream, telling him to go to the house of Saul. Ananias, rebutted, "This man who has done so much evil to the saints at Jerusalem?" Verse 15 records, "But the Lord said unto him, go thy way: for he is a chosen vessel unto me, to bear my name before the Gentiles, and kings, and the children of Israel".

The Bible is clear, God/Holy Spirit calls and appoints leaders to ministry, not man. The church also has a part to play in the process by endorsing what God is doing.

Acts 13:1-3 records the church in Antioch as it ordained Saul and Barnabas. **1**"Now there were in the church that was at Antioch certain prophets and teachers; as Barnabas, and Simeon that was called Niger, and Lucius of Cyrene, and Manaen, which had been brought up with Herod the tetrarch, and Saul.

2 As they ministered to the Lord, and fasted, **the Holy Ghost said, separate me Barnabas and Saul for the work whereunto I have called them**.

3 And when they had fasted and prayed and laid their hands on them, they sent them away."

Notice, it is the Holy Ghost who chose the candidates for ordination or for separation to a specific order or station of service. The Holy Ghost said, "separate for me". Verse 17 of the same chapter says, "The God of this people **of Israel chose our fathers**, and exalted the people when they dwelt as strangers in the land of Egypt, and with a high arm brought he them out of it."

Ordination is God's foreknowledge at work in choosing us to be part of his plan, even before we were conceived. The first step toward ordination is initiated by God. God breathes on anything that will be accepted and used by him. Therefore, a theology of ordination begins with the recognition that the Holy Spirit is already at work giving spiritual birth to the believer, quickening her or him to spiritual things and then equipping that one with spiritual fruits and gifts for service. The church then gives acknowledgement to this manifestation. The second and most important step is the role of the church in the process as a local group or congregation. The church endorses what God has already birthed and made manifest, i.e., the gift of leadership, singing, exhortation, preaching etc. The first step can be classified as qualification and the second confirmation, neither is gender-based.

Finally, verse 48 of Acts chapter 13 says "And when the Gentiles heard this, they were glad, and glorified the word of the Lord: and as many as were ordained to eternal life believed." The church or human beings cannot ordain anyone to eternal life, only God can. Therefore, the word ordain connotes an action on the part of divinity, not humanity. Ordination, theologically speaking is the act of God in manifesting his grace to a believer in choosing her or him to be a part of God's salvation and salvific activity.

A renowned and influential 19th-century female church founder and leader, Ellen G. White said, "**The Lord ordained me as His messenger.**"[86] She was an activist for gender inclusiveness in the church and penned the same to male leaders at the highest level of the organisation even though she was not confirmed by the church as ordained. However, her pointed statement above is indicative of her understanding that ordination is God's doing, and the church would do well to get its theology right.

---

[86] Review and Herald, May 18, (1911). https://m. egwwritings.org/search?lang=en&query=the+lord+ordained+me+as+his+messenger&suggestion=0. (Accessed September 18, 2022).

The service churches preside over, called ordination, is the realisation and confirmation (not even authorisation) of the working of God in the life of one called by God. The church members and their leaders acknowledge God's calling on a fellow believer through prayer/laying on of hands and a given assignment to ministry according to the believer's gift(s) or a missional need. (This we call ordination). Ordination is not man's doing as much as we would like to think so; it is God's appointment in which men may play a part. (See Acts 13: 2-4.) I say, in which men may play a part because, Bible characters and other believers have said, "The Lord ordained me" without a ceremony by the church. However, to maintain order, transparency and for accountability, the church keeps a record of all those it sends to minister and issues a credential, accordingly which is quite in order.

A faulty theology about women

We have often begun the conversation about ordination in the wrong place. We have approached this divine phenomenon from the human standpoint of the church (ecclesia) and its power to confer a rite on believers, whereas, the Bible's first mention of ordination is a calling always initiated by God, not the church. The Holy Spirit (pneuma) in His sovereign will predestines and moves on individuals birthing His purposes. Like in the case of Jeremiah, ordination commenced before his conception and birth; it was not a human appointment. Does the Church want to take credit for what the Holy Spirit does? I don't think so.

Though very important, the church only bears witness to what the Holy Spirit is doing in the believer's life, and its authority lies only as it works with the Holy Spirit. Ordination is not a sacrament the church grants to a worthy qualifier based on class, race, education, gender or the like. It is not a human phenomenon that one mortal confers upon another; it is what God initiated long before the ordinant themself came into existence and began participating in God's divine and sovereign will.

The church's position that a woman should not be ordained is unbiblical and a serious affront to God's omniscience, omnipotence and sovereignty. Putting it mildly, it is discriminatory and misogynistic and putting it frankly, blasphemous by trying to deface the image of God in women and to belittle or devalue women's work.

The root of discrimination against women

The arguments of an ontological difference between man and woman at creation or the limitation and subordination of women because of Eve's role in the entrance of sin as reasons for women to be deemed unworthy to be equally included in all aspects of the grace and mission of the church are erroneous, unsubstantiated, defamatory, irrelevant, misogynistic, sexist and distracting from the beautiful work that God accomplishes in the lives of women and men, through His Spirit.

That woman was created second as a "helpmeet"; that Eve sinned first and not Adam; and that women should keep silent in the churches and not speak or exercise authority, has often been cited as the basis for excluding women from being ordained and holding certain leadership positions in the church. Truth be told, the issue of women's ordination is a smoke screen! Why? The origins and etymology of the word and practice of ordination have nothing to do with gender. There is sufficient textual evidence to support that God commissions/calls and sets aside/ordains both males and females.

The church above all has been doubly admonished by the same Apostle Paul to "Study to shew thyself approved unto God, a workman that needeth not to be ashamed, rightly dividing the word of truth". 2 Timothy 2:15. In the first instance, **the church has been called to study**; to deploy proper exegetical skills, examining the *Sitz im Leben* and in the second instance, **"Rightly divide the word of truth",** that is the work of doing hermeneutics, deciphering not only what is said, but what is meant and how it should be applied. On these two counts the church has failed; to "study" and to "rightly divide the word of truth", hence, we are in this dilemma of barring women from being ordained and a host of other discriminatory ideologies and practices instigated and perpetuated by a male-dominated clergy.

The Church should repent for its neglect to "Study" and to "Rightly divide the word of truth". The Church should apologise to women for the ill treatment that women have received for millennia, because of the misinterpretation of the scriptures.

Because of not understanding the scriptures and how the Holy Spirit functions, the erroneous theology about women, sin, salvation and the nature of the church have permeated the teachings of the Protestant and the Roman Catholic churches which effectively have debarred women from ever becoming a Pope, Archbishop, Cardinal, or Priest, or an ordained pastor, simply because they are female.

In the Protestant Church, women serve in almost every layer and category of leadership; they perform the same tasks as their male counterparts. Still, in many denominations, a woman will not be considered for ordination based on:

1. The ontological argument, that (By nature or ontology) Eve as a helpmeet meant that she was less than equal by nature.

2. The pre-eminence argument, that (Adam was created 1st and Eve 2nd).

3. The subordination argument, that (Eve's role in the entrance of sin meant that men would rule over all women is disputed in Chapter 1).

4. Apostle Paul's controversial prohibition, that women should not speak or exercise authority. (a misapplication of the Apostle's words, motives and stance on women)

To be candid, we don't need to go any further on the ordination issue because we've seen that the conversation on

ordination began with the wrong question, should the church ordain women? An ecclesiastical question the church answers with a no, so the church feels justified in its stated position. The church backed up this question with an answer from a non-biblical definition of ordination and a faulty exegesis of the Apostle Paul's sayings about women; consequently, we have spent centuries debating the issue as to whether women should be ordained. The church does not ordain anyone; according to the Bible, the Holy Spirit does. (Jeremiah 1:5) The Holy Spirit gives gifts to whomsoever he wills. The prophet Joel confirmed that the "whomsoever" includes women, "And it shall come to pass afterward, that I will pour out my spirit upon all flesh; and your sons and your daughters shall prophesy" Joel 2:28. Therefore, the church does not have biblical authority to bar women who have been gifted by the Holy Spirit from exercising their calling. To so do is blatant discrimination.

We can be opinionated on any subject; however, on ethical and moral issues and theological doctrines, we begin with what the Word of God says; what the Holy Spirit has revealed, and if in any doubt, we examine what Jesus taught and did. The Word of God is evident, God made male and female in his image and likeness; He poured out his spirit on women in the Old Testament and further promised to continue that trajectory in the last days as prophesied in Joel 2:28.

We have seen the gift of the Holy Spirit working in both the Old and New Testaments through the gift of prophecy, exonerated through the lives of 10 righteous prophetesses (female prophets). The prophet or prophetess had more authority than the king because all understood that they derived their status from God himself. They would say to a king, "Thus saith the Lord" and that was seen as authoritative. Jesus had many female followers, and He commissioned Mary as the first female evangelist with the Good News of the resurrection to "Go tell Peter and the disciples" that he rose. Please, church leaders, be honest with the scriptures.

There should be no discrimination along the lines of gender in the church, rather, the same equality that exists in the Godhead must be characterised in the relationships within the body of Christ, the church.

In the Old Testament times, in what was considered a patriarchal society, we see women empowered by the Holy Spirit to be Prophets, Judges, Queens and leaders. Human conventions or strictures did not determine the work of the Holy Spirit then, and neither should it now. The Holy Spirit can move upon things, animate or inanimate to accomplish their divine purpose. To imply that God has somehow restricted himself to using men only and not women who were equally made in their image to reflect their glory, despite evidence to the contrary, is just preposterous and misogynistic. God's thoughts are not our thoughts, nor are his ways our ways.

The Holy Spirit, one of the primary movers in the creation of the universe is the primary initiator and supplier of gifts for the work of the church-the spiritual kingdom. The Apostle Paul confirms the initiative of the Holy Spirit in the operations of the church in the New Testament as it was in the Old, "There are different gifts, but the same Spirit. There are different ways of working, but the same God works all things in all people." (No gender differentiation) 1 Cor. 12:4-6. "All these are the work of one and the same Spirit, and he distributes them to each one, just as he determines."1 Cor: 12:11 (As He determines, it did not say, according to gender). "But in fact, God has arranged the members of the body, every one of them, according to His design." 1 Cor. 12:18. (If we are to take the word "design," literally?) Genesis tells us that God's design is, male and female made in their image of oneness and equality).

Could the Bible be more explicit than that? That the abilities of believers are gifts from God, given to males and females alike? Who then gives the church the prerogative to say that it should not recognise the gift of leadership demonstrated in a woman's life because she is female? How did we get there? Could we undermine the authority of the scriptures above? Should not scripture rather than culture, inform our practice? Should we not desist from putting a masculine construct on the word ordination and accept the biblical teaching that the Holy Spirit calls both males and females? The church should not dither over what the Spirit does.

Churches need to be theological and not ecclesiological about ordination; yes, we may require academic qualifications for denominational employment and that is understood, but ordination is not a sacrament that the church dispenses to whomever it decides to qualify. Ordination in the Bible is the calling of God on the lives of believers manifested in gifts and ministries for kingdom business, let ordination remain in the spiritual realm and not in the academic or sociological. **The church must prayerfully and confidently recognise the divine calling of a believer through prayer and blessing or laying on of hands, male and female alike, end of the story. This is biblical ordination; anything less or more than this that the church practices are nothing more than an ecclesiastical pronouncement unauthorised by the Holy Spirit.**

The rest of this chapter will set out the etymology of the troubled word-ordination and further clarify the anomaly of women's exclusion from the ordained clergy of the church.

Definition of Ordination

First, let us look at the definition of ordination in general and then we will look at ordination in its ecclesiastical sense.

According to the International Standard Bible Encyclopedia:

> **ORDINATION or-di-na-shun** (Latin ordinare, to set in order & to arrange: to appoint to; from ordo, order; arrangement).

> Ordination: The act of arranging in regular order, especially the act of investing with ministerial or sacerdotal rank (ordo), the setting apart for an office in the Christian ministry. The word does not occur in the

English Version of the Bible."[87]

According to Webster's Revised Unabridged Dictionary:

Ordain: In the King James Version, the verb to ordain renders as many as 35 different words (11 Hebrew words in the Old Testament, 21 Greek words in Apocrypha and the New Testament, and 3 Latin words in Apocrypha). This is because the English word has many shades of meaning (especially as used at the time the King James Version was made) as set out below:

(1) To set in order, arrange, and prepare:

1 Chronicle 17:9 (the Revised Version), Psalms 7:13 (the Revised Version (British and American), Habakkuk 1:12 (also the Revised Version (British and American)).

(2) To establish, institute, and bring into being:

When this order (i.e., the Garter) was ordained, my Lord; (Shakespeare). In 1 Kings 12:32, Jeroboam ordained a feast in the 8th month (12:33); Numbers 28:6; Psalms 8:2,3; Isaiah 26:12; 2 Esdras 6:49 the King James Version (the Revised Version (British and American) Galatians 3:19.

(3) To decree, give orders, prescribe:

And doth the Power that man adores Ordain their doom. See Esther 9:27.

The Jews ordained that they would keep these two days according to the writing thereof; 1 Esdras 6:34; 2 Esdras 7:17; 8:14 the King James Version; Tobit 1:6; Additions to Esther 14:9; 1 Macc 4:59; 7:49; Acts 16:4; Romans 7:10 the King James Version;1 Corinthians 2:7; 7:17; 9:14; Ephesians 2:10 the King James Version.

---

[87]https://www.biblestudytools.com/dictionary/ordain-ordination/. (Accessed September 25, 2022).

(4) To set apart for an office or duty, appoint, destine:

(5) To appoint ceremonially to the ministerial or priestly office, to confer holy orders on. This later technical or ecclesiastical sense is never found in English Versions of the Bible. The nearest approach is (4) above, but the idea of a formal or ceremonial setting apart from the office (prominent in its modern usage) is never implied in the word.[88]

According to Strong's Concordance, the word ordain comes from the root word "Tásso":

5021 *tássō* – properly, *arrange* (put in order); to place in a *particular order, appoint*; (figuratively) ordain, set in place; "station" (J. Thayer).

5021 */tássō* ("place in position, post") was commonly used in ancient military language for "*designating*" ("*appointing*, commissioning") *a specific status*, i.e. arranging (placing) in a deliberate, fixed order.

[5021 (*tássō*) was "primarily a military term meaning 'to draw up in order, arrange in place, assign, appoint, order." [89]

ORDINATION IN THE NEW TESTAMENT

"During the first millennium of Christianity, ordination meant election by and installation of a person to perform a particular function in a Christian community. Not only bishops, priests, deacons and subdeacons but also porters, lectors, exorcists, acolytes, canons, abbots, abbesses, kings, queens and empresses were all considered equally ordained. This makes perfect sense. An *ordo* (order) was a group in the church (or society) that had a particular job or vocation. Any job or vocation

---

[88] https://www.biblehub.com/topical/o/ordain. htm. (Accessed September 25, 2022).
[89] https://biblehub.com/greek/5021.htm (Accessed December 30, 2022).

was called an "order," and the process by which one was chosen and designated for that vocation was an "ordination." The meaning of ordination and how women were gradually excluded."[90]

In the New Testament, according to D. Miall Edwards, "Ordination, was regarded as an outward act of approval, a symbolic offering of intercessory prayer, and an emblem of the solidarity of the Christian community, rather than a rite particularly aimed at a certain gender. It did not connote some mystical, indispensable channel of grace for the work of the church."[91]

The following article is a direct quote from D. Miall Edward on Ordination:

> *The New Testament does not throw much light on the modern ecclesiastical rite of ordination. The 12 disciples were not set apart by any formal action on the part of Jesus. In Mark 3:14; John 15:16, the King James Version rendering ordain is, nothing more than an appointment or election. In John 20:21-23, we have a symbolic act of consecration, "He breathed on them", but the act is described as a one-off and not repeated.*

> *In the Apostolic age, there is no trace of the doctrine of an outward rite conferring inward grace. However, we have instances of the formal appointment or recognition of those who had already given proof of their spiritual qualification.*

> *The Seven were chosen by the brethren as men already full of the Spirit and of wisdom and were then appointed by the Twelve, who prayed and laid their hands upon them (Acts 6:1-6).*

---

[90] https://www.ncronline.org/news/meaning-ordination-and-how-women-were-gradually-excluded. January 16, 2013. Gary Macy. (Accessed May 12, 2022).
[91] https://www.internationalstandardbible.com/O/ordain-ordination.html. (Accessed October 10, 2021).

The call of Barnabas and Saul came directly from God (Acts 13:2, the work whereupon I have called them; Acts 13:4, they were sent forth by the Holy Spirit). Yet certain prophets and teachers were instructed by the Holy Spirit to separate them (i.e., publicly) for their work, which they did by fasting and praying and laying on of hands (Acts 13:3). But Paul did not regard the church's act as constituting him an apostle. "Paul, an apostle, not of men, neither by man, but by Jesus Christ, and God the Father, who raised him from the dead" Galatians 1:1.

*Barnabas and Paul are said to have ordained the elders or presbyters in every city with prayers and fasting (Acts 14:23). Titus was instructed by Paul to appoint elders in every city in Crete (Titus 1:5). To the same effect, **Christ assures His apostles that it was not they who had chosen Him, but He who had chosen and appointed them (John 15:16); and Paul admonishes the Ephesian elders to take heed to all the flock over which the Holy Spirit had made them bishops or overseers (Acts 20:28).** In the Pastoral Epistles, Paul refers to the charism which was given to Timothy by prophetic utterance when the elders laid their hands on him (1 Tim. 4:14; cf. 5:22; 2 Tim. 1:6) and instructs Titus to appoint elders in every town of Crete (Titus 1:5). Within the biblical perspective, then, ordination is primarily an act of God's calling and appointment, and only secondarily an act of the church, which by prayer seeks to know and follow the will of God.*

The gift of Timothy for evangelistic work seems to have been formally recognized in two ways:

    (a) by the laying on of the hands of the presbytery (1 Timothy 4:14),

    (b) by the laying on of the hands of Paul himself (2 Timothy 1:6).

The words Lay hands hastily on no man (1 Timothy

5:22) do not refer to an act of ordination, but probably to the restoration of the penitent.? The reference in Hebrews 6:2 is not exclusively to ordination, but to all occasions of laying on of hands.

From the few instances mentioned above (the only ones found in the New Testament), we infer that it was regarded as advisable that persons holding high office in the church should be publicly recognized in some way, such as by laying on of hands, fasting, and public prayer. But no great emphasis was laid on this rite, hence, it can hardly be likely that any essential principle was held to be involved in; (Hort, The Christian Ecclesia, 216).[92]

Ministerial Appointment in the New Testament

The twelve disciples of Jesus were male, but this was not a template for the future selection of disciples, it was not prescriptive but descriptive. Jesus also had many female disciples or followers and for obvious reasons, they were not itinerant. For those with a narrow conception that maleness constitutes a disciple, here is what Jesus says, "Then said Jesus to those Jews which believed on him, **if ye continue in my word, *then* are ye my disciples indeed**;" John 8:31. A disciple is simply put, one who continues in the word or is obedient to Jesus' instruction. Another definition of a disciple is one who has love for others, "By this shall all men know that **ye are my disciples if ye have love one to another**." John 13:35.

We must resist the temptation and move away from making a model or formulating a theology from statements in the Bible that were descriptive rather than prescriptive. A disciple is a follower of Jesus be they male or female, upon whom God declared that He would pour out his spirit. (Joel 2:28).

---

92. Ibid.

Consistent with the Old Testament, the New Testament affirms firstly, that God is the one who chooses. **"Ye have not chosen me, but I have chosen you, and ordained you, that ye should go and bring forth fruit, and that your fruit should remain".** John 15:16. Acts chapter 13:2-4, records a New Testament ordination, "While they were worshipping the Lord and fasting, the Holy Spirit said, 'Set apart for me Barnabas and Saul for the work to which I have called them.' Firstly, it is the Holy Spirit who said, "set them apart". Secondly, the church in tune with the Holy Spirit, obeys the Spirit and lays hands on them or simply turns to God who has shown up in equipping the saints. Thirdly, the Holy Spirit sends them on their way. Who sends them off? The Holy Spirit.

Yes, God works through the church, but it is the Holy Spirit that calls, equips and ordains or sets people apart for ministry, and the same Holy Spirit is apparent in going ahead of, and along with the ordinant, to bring conviction or lift Jesus through the ministry of the one being sent. "The wind bloweth where it listeth, and thou hearest the sound thereof, but canst not tell whence it cometh, and whither it goeth: so is everyone that is born of the Spirit." John 3:8. Although the phrase "everyone" is written in the nominative masculine singular, it refers to every kind, anyone and or, every person who the Spirit calls."[93]

Paul and Barnabas directed the appointment of elders "in each church" Acts 14:23. He instructed Titus to "appoint elders in every town" Titus 1:5. In the above passages, the appointment of elders involved the whole congregation. In other words, a local congregation recognised the calling and gifts of a member, and the members endorsed their ordination.

"The Greek word used in 2 Corinthians 8:19 for Titus's appointment and Acts 14:23 for the choosing of the Galatian elders means "to stretch forth the hands." It was a word normally used for the act of voting in the Athenian

---

[93] The Gospel of John original Greek text and translation at: https://www.gospel-john.com/chapter-3/. (Accessed September 18, 2022).

legislature. Thus, the ordination of church leaders involved a consensus in the church, if not an official vote. The apostles and the congregations knew whom the Spirit had chosen, and they responded by placing those persons in leadership. When God calls and qualifies a believer for the ministry, it will be apparent both to that person and to the rest of the church."[94]

Certification of leaders by the church is important today. As an organisation develops, it sets into place its leadership structure; this helps to preserve the integrity of teaching, order and proper administration. As the early church expanded into a network of believers, it needed the resources of itinerant Elders. Therefore, it was important for the congregations local and distant to certify that those who were leading out were bona fide.

"The modern definition of ordination as "the investiture of clergy" or "the act of granting pastoral authority or sacerdotal power," is not biblical. Usually, we think of an ordination service as a ceremony in which someone is commissioned or appointed to a position within the church. Often, the ceremony involves the laying on of hands."[95]

"The word ordain in the Bible refers to a setting in place or designation; for example, Joseph was "ordained" as a ruler in Egypt (Acts 7:10); the steward in Jesus' parable was "ordained" to oversee a household (Matthew 24:45); deacons were "ordained" to serve the Jerusalem church (Acts 6:1-6), and pastors were "ordained" in each city in Crete (Titus 1:5). In none of these cases is the mode of ordination specified, nor is any ceremony detailed; the "ordinations" are simply appointments."[96]

Female Deacons were ordained in the New Testament.

"The New Testament gives an example of a woman who was

---

[94] What does the Bible say about ordination Your Questions. Biblical Answers: https://www.gotquestions.org/ordination.html. (Accessed August 30, 2022).
[95] https://www.gotquestions.org/ordination. html#ixzz2ZAcoMieb. (Accessed on 10 October, 2022).
[96] Ibid.

appointed as a deacon. "Paul inserts a brief list of qualifications for female deacons, sometimes translated as the "wives" of the deacons (1 Tim 3:11; NIV). The Greek simply says, "Women likewise dignified . . ." In other words, Paul does not seem to be referring here to the deacons' wife but to women appointed to the deacons' role."[97]

In Rom 16:1, St. Paul recommends a female deacon, "I commend to you our sister Phoebe, a servant {or deacon} of the church in Cenchrea." "What we have here is the common elements of Greco-Roman epistolary commendations: "Duff states that the mention of letters of recommendation by Paul in 2 Cor. 3:1-3 'strongly suggests that the community had indeed requested letters of recommendation as a guarantee of Paul's honesty."[98] The request, "That ye receive her in the Lord, as becometh saints" is a huge undertaking by Paul, putting himself and his credibility as an apostle, on the line. "And that ye assist her in whatsoever business she hath need of you: for she hath been a succourer of many, and of myself also", confirms Paul's willingness to guarantee or stand by the bearer of the letter.

"Phoebe did not just carry Paul's letter: she delivered it. Punctuation had not yet been invented to indicate how the text should be read, so couriers likely read letters aloud to the recipients, mimicking the author's tone of voice and facial expressions. Phoebe would probably have rehearsed the letter with Paul, noting where he spoke with sarcasm or sadness and where his eyes rolled or flashed with intensity. This was especially important because Paul had not yet visited the Christians in Rome, so they would not know how he spoke when he preached. Paul commended Phoebe so the Christians in Rome would know that he trusted her to read his letter precisely the

[97] Jean Daniélou, The Ministry of Women in the Early Church, Faith Press, Leighton Buzzard (1974), p. 14.

[98] Paul B. Duff, Moses in Corinth: The Apologetic Context of 2 Corinthians 3 (NovTSup, 159; Leiden, Brill: 2015), pp. 103-15, quoted in, David I Yoon, ANCIENT LETTERS OF RECOMMENDATION AND 2 CORINTHIANS 3.1-3: A LITERARY ANALYSIS, (2016) p. 48.

way he wanted them to hear it."[99]

"In the Roman Empire, no postal service was available for everyone to use. Therefore, if you wanted to send a letter, you had to find someone to deliver it. Paul regularly dispatched his co-workers for this very purpose: to deliver his letters and to serve as his representatives and the letters' first interpreters for the communities that received them.

> In the case of the letter to the Romans, Phoebe was sent to Rome with Paul's letter. Members of the Roman community were no doubt full of questions after it was read. Phoebe was the person who would answer their questions and explain further what Paul meant due to her first-hand knowledge of Paul's message and her experience of serving the gospel alongside him as a co-worker. Phoebe was the first interpreter of Paul's letter to the Romans". A man who believed women should not speak in the church would never have done that." Romans 16: Who was Phoebe?."[100]

"Notice Paul's references to women leaders he mentions and recommends, "Greet Prisca and Aquila my fellow workers in Christ Jesus'... 'Greet Mary who has worked so much among you.' In the same way 'Tryphena, Tryphosa and Persis labour in the Lord.' Romans 16,1-16. Euodia and Syntyche who have struggled together with me in the Gospel with Clement and the rest of my fellow workers." Philippians 4:2. According to John Wijngaards, 'In the Gospel' certainly implies participation in the work of evangelism.

Compare also: "The apostles, giving themselves without respite to the work of evangelism as befitted their

---

[99] "Making Peace with Paul," the Spring 2021 issue of Mutuality magazine. https://www.cbeinternational.org/resource/article/mutuality. - blog-magazine/phoebe-through-eyes-paul. (September 12, 2022).
[100] 92   April 25, 2017, Jen McNeel. http://thetextincontext.com/romans-16-who-wasphoebe/. (Accessed 08, 2022).

ministry, took with them women, not as wives but as sisters, to share in their ministry to women living at home: by their agency, the teaching of the Lord reached the women's quarters without arousing suspicion'. Clement of Alexandria, Stromata 3, 6, §53.

In a letter to the emperor (111 AD), Pliny mentions that he arrested two Christian women who held an official position. "All the more it seemed necessary to me to find out the truth from these two slave women, who were called 'ancillae' [=diakonous, deaconesses?], even by applying torture.

And compare the story of Thecla, who, by her confession before the judge at Antioch, converted Tryphaena and a group of women. 'She went to Tryphaena's house and stayed there for eight days, instructing her in the Word of God, so that most of her servants believed'."[101] Women actively taught in house groups and formed 'churches' in their homes.

The Church Fathers and the Middle Ages

The theology of the Church of the Middle Ages was pretty nuanced. **"According to the theology of the Middle Ages, the faithful become recipients of grace through the church's sacraments. The priest or clergy were crucial in this process in maintaining mediaeval patriarchy, with only the males acting as mediators between God and the people dispensing grace and forgiveness."[102]**

"Luther challenged this practice and asserted that all believers enjoyed direct access to God and that there is no

---

[101] (Acts of Paul and Thecla, § 38-39). John Wijngaards. https://www.womendeacons.org/history/deac_his. shtml. (Accessed 15, 2022).
[102] Pierce, Ronald W. Groothuis, Rebecca Merrill Fee, Gordon D. p. 275.

human mediator except Christ; that one receives God's grace directly and has the privilege of coming to God for themselves."[103] Hence, he posted the 95 Theses, which were based on the three main tenets of the Protestant Reformation: sola fide; sola gratis; sola scriptura.

"St Thomas Aquinas, in his development of Roman Catholic theology, said that the priest is representative of Christ at the Eucharist, and so it is widely held in Roman Catholic circles that not only the bread becomes the body of Christ, but that the priest in person is our lord. According to Roman Catholic theology, in pronouncing the words of consecration at the Eucharist, the priest takes the representational role of Christ to the point of being his very image; hence a woman will not be ordained to the priesthood in Roman Catholicism."[104]

"The Roman Catholic tradition is steeped in replacing the sacrifice of Christ with the institutional role of the priests. Many Protestants do not believe in an institutional role for pastors or ministers, rather they see the church as the Laos: the body of Christ. Pastors are not mediators between God and man, they are not a special class of Christians who mediate God's grace to the people. Simply put, ordained Pastors and Ministers are people chosen by God and recognised by the church and charged with the responsibility of utilising their spiritual giftedness in leading men and women to Christ."[105]

"Of course, Protestants do not accept the Roman Catholic Church's theology of the Mass but have been influenced by such teaching by insisting that women would be unsuitable to lead in Holy Communion. The officiant in a communion service or at the Lord's Supper does not fulfil the representational function, they do not perform that priestly function or take the place of Christ. The priest, the bread and the wine are just visual representations, not substitutes or replicas. An all-male clergy perpetuates the idea that the Eucharist is a Mass in which a

---

[103] Ibid., p. 276.
[104] Ibid., p. 279.
[105] Ibid., p. 277.

priest acts like Christ. Extending the Old Testament model of male priesthood fails to recognise the priestly functions of Jesus Christ in his once and for all sacrifice for men and the new covenant which he inaugurated."[106]

For those who would argue against women leading as pastors based on the representational character of the male priests as representing Christ, (Pierce and Groothuis 279) let me state that it was not Christ's maleness that saved us, it was not his gender, Jesus became flesh, (Anthropos) human not (aner) male. He came in the likeness of all He intended to save, male and female alike. "What the son did not assume in the incarnation he could not redeem."[107] It was Jesus's sinless life as a result of his unbroken relationship with his father that saved us, not his gender.

One of the effects of representational theology is what I call the stain of institutional patriarchy wherein, many women feel a sense of inadequacy, or unsuitability to be a minister, they feel that somehow a woman is not good enough to carry out such functions. The impact of institutional patriarchy is a picture of a masculine image to occupy the role of the minister or priest so that a woman does not see herself as being able to step into a gendered space.

"Before the 1960s the millennia-long teaching of the church was that women, though equally saved, were intrinsically unequal to men. Based especially on a misreading of 1 Tim 2:14 ("Adam was not deceived, but Eve was and became a transgressor") and 1 Cor 11:7 ("he is the image and glory of God; but woman is the glory of man"), the major figures of church history believed that women were made of "lesser stuff" than men—they were less intelligent and capable than men, and more prone to instability and deception. It was therefore assumed that men should lead women for their own good."[108]

---

[106] Ibid., p. 279-280.
[107] Ibid., p. 281.
[108] CBE International, https://www.cbeinternational. org/resource/subordinating-jesus-and-women-and-how-influential-

Bearing in mind the negative and demeaning way women were caricatured by eminent Church Fathers and philosophers like, Augustine and Aristotle, it is not surprising that Christian theology has been influenced by these notions and deeply held distorted beliefs about women.

I must also remind you of where we started; at the beginning where man and woman were equally created in the image of Christ, therefore, a woman has that representational element of Christ by creation, anyhow. There's no ontological difference between the male and the female in God's sight. "In the image of God created he them, male and female created he them" And God is neither male nor female. "Although the incarnation (the birth of Jesus) in the form of a male may have been historically and culturally necessary, attaching soteriological necessity to this would undercut Christ's status as representing all humans; male and female in salvation."[109]

Rhetorical/preaching spaces

Female ministers contend with millennia of traditions, beliefs and expectations that have been built around the gendered space-the pulpit, which to a large extent has been endorsed and customised as a male space.

The traditionally styled lecterns found in many churches were undoubtedly designed with men in mind, implicitly, they lend to the subconscious messages of status and gender hierarchy. Even when a woman occupies the pulpit, in many minds, a male figure is still expected. By revamping the pulpit space, which was often distant from the pew and elevated above the congregants, the preacher can emit more sincerity, rapport and identification with the congregation when preaching from spaces that are not gendered. [110]

Roxanne Mountford defines the rhetorical space or preaching

evangelical-teachers-led-us-astray/. (Accessed September 28, 2022).
[109] Pierce, Ronald W. Groothuis, Rebecca Merrill Fee, Gordon D. p. 282.
[110] Roxanne Mountford, The Gendered Pulpit: Preaching in American Protestant Spaces (Carbondale: Southern Illinois UP, 2003) 16-23.

space as architecturally and culturally, gendered.[111] She points out that the pulpit has historically been a space of male dominance and was designed to separate the minister and the congregation, alluding to the gender hierarchy referenced in 1 Corinthians 11:3. Mountford asserts, "Rhetorical space is an extraordinarily important aspect of rhetorical performance . . . where each object and participant is set in place according to the rituals."[112] She contends that the rhetorical pulpit space is marked "by reinforcing the idea that the pulpit is the sacred place where godly men preach."[113] "The arts of preaching, among the oldest of the rhetorical arts, inscribes this masculine tradition on the pages of preaching manuals, sometimes explicitly but most often through a smooth surface of universal advice untroubled by the specificity of gender."[114] " Preaching is fundamentally an act of rhetorical performance, the gendered nature of that performance (voice, gesture, and movement) virtually reinforcing a congregation's belief."[115]

Carol Norén, in her book "The Woman in the Pulpit", explains that some feminists believe that not only the rhetorical space but the liturgical materials, whether intentional or not, "reflect the passivity of women and the dominance of men."[116] These feminists, she further stipulates, assert that "The oppressiveness of mainline liturgical patterns is more than a matter of masculine names and metaphors; it is a sacralisation of patriarchal history in scripture and tradition. It embraces imperial and hierarchical orderings of groups of people."[117]

The historical expectations of the preaching space being

---

[111] Ibid., p. 17.
[112] Ibid., p. 37.
[113] Ibid., p. 34.
[114] Ibid., p. 2.
[115] Ibid., p. 4.
[116] Carol Norén, The Woman in the Pulpit (Nashville: Abingdon, 1991), 154. See also Janet R. Walton, "The Challenge of Feminist Liturgy," Liturgy: Journal of Liturgical Conference 6, no. 1 (1986, The Church and Culture), p. 556.
[117] Ibid., p. 154.

occupied by a male have led to extremely strong, reprehensible and castigating comments about women ministers. Also, hostility by women, to other women who become pastors is extremely caustic and toxic. It also comes at a high price.

Prejudice and hostility to women by women and by males, inflict a high level of hazard, mental stress and physical illnesses on women. It's a very demeaning type of discrimination to be rejected and not accepted by those of your own 'household'. Women leaders face a type of hostility that their male counterparts know not of. They are challenged at their very core for being female. Many female ministers and non-church leaders, battle with stress-related illnesses that are directly related to denial of their gifts and talents.

We need to protect our women leaders from discriminatory practices and policies and the churches need to help our women leaders to cope with injustices. Foremost, however, religious communities and society, must call out the sin of misogyny and discrimination against women, be it, female on female or male on female. By declaring the biblical theology of women as exegeted in this book along with a refutation of the arguments that have been traditionally used to support the evil of discrimination against women, we are well-armed to end this pandemic.

Ordination in the context of the church

We should consider the context in which ordination occurs; therefore, we need to briefly discuss the nature and function of the church.

The New Testament concept of the 'saved ones' is referred to as the church, the Ecclesia, (Greek-Ekklesia): 'the ones called out' who form the Laos-the body of Christ. The Apostle Peter in 1 Peter 2:9 refers to "the ones called out" as a chosen generation, a royal priesthood. Paul refers to them as the body of Christ in 1 Corinthians chapter 12. **In the first instance, we must** remember that the church is called to reflect the essence of God (Elohim) or their image: love reflected in oneness and equality. Love, oneness and equality express God's image and character to the world. We see the Holy Spirit empowering church members with gifts without reference or distinction to ethnicity, race or gender, circumcision or uncircumcision. The Spirit gives gifts to whomsoever He wills: a genderless distribution of gifts for the building up of the body for effective witnessing to the love, oneness and equality of God to the entire world. This, in summary, is our understanding of the mission and function of the church. For "By this {witness of love manifested in unity and equality amongst each other,} shall all men know that ye are my disciples." John 13:35 (revised by the author)

The church comprises men and women whom the Holy Spirit has called, saved, gifted, sent, or commissioned, in short, ordained by God. Whether the church acknowledges the endorsement of the Holy Spirit or not, it is the Holy Spirit who calls or ordains and equips women and men to the ministry. This calling is their ordination. In real terms, therefore, the church recognises and endorses the same. Probably, our phraseology should be thus, MEMBER X HAS BEEN ORDAINED OF GOD, CONSEQUENTLY, AS A CHURCH, WE WOULD LIKE TO FORMALLY RECOGNIZE THIS BY APPOINTING MEMBER X TO SERVE AS A DEACON OR IN A PARTICULAR NAMED MINISTRY. In effect, what we are saying is that God ordains an individual according to his omniscience and the church certifies, appoints, sets apart or commissions them.

The Seventh-day Adventist Church (SDA)

Like many other Christian Churches, the SDA Church recognises the role of women in ministry but does not grant them full ecclesiastical authority, as in ordination, although it ordains females to other ministries within the church. (An anomaly) The result is a male-exclusive ordained ministerial team in a church that is over 60 percent female. Women are restricted in the exercise of their calling and giftedness and by default, are excluded from having input in decision-making at a level which affects the lives of millions of women in the church. Left the way it is, it means that at the time of going to press with this manuscript, a woman will not be considered to be a Conference, Union, Division or General Conference President, which is discriminatory. (However, I believe that this will soon change).

This issue of parity for women in ministry has engrossed the minds of church administrators for well over a century. Here was the church's rationale for ordination as stated on the 24th November 1879, by Elder G. I. Butler, President:

"ORDINATION

WHEREAS, Certain difficulties in the past in connection with this cause have grown out of the subject of ordination, arising from the question, who is authorized to baptize and administer the other ordinances of the church? and

WHEREAS, In the rapid growth of this cause, these difficulties will probably increase, as it extends to other people and draws from other denominations ministers and official members, and

WHEREAS, It is very desirable that some uniform plan of action should be adopted by our different conferences and ministers in all parts of the field; and as our work has reached that stage where some action on this subject is eminently desirable, therefore

RESOLVED, *That to meet this want we express the opinion as the sense of this Conference, that none but those who are Scripturally ordained are properly qualified to administer baptism and other ordinances.*"[118]

It certainly makes a lot of sense that the organization took

---

[118] General Conference Session 63-88, 162-163 (http://www.adventistarchives.org/docs/GCB/GCB1863-88.pdf#view=fit). (Accessed October 26, 2022).

steps to certify persons who administered the ordinances of the church, through ordination certification. The purpose was to maintain a certain level of accountability. Very clearly, ordination became the means to identify bona fide or authorised personnel, with nothing to do with gender. Here is further corroboration of this:

"God foresaw the difficulties that His servants would be called to meet, and, in order that their work should be above challenge, He instructed the church by revelation to set them apart publicly to the work of the ministry. Their ordination was a public recognition of their divine appointment to bear to the Gentiles the glad tidings of the gospel. Both Paul and Barnabas had already received their commission from God Himself, and the ceremony of the laying on of hands added no new grace or virtual qualification. At a later date, the rite of ordination by the laying on of hands was greatly abused; unwarrantable importance was attached to the act, as if a power came at once upon those who received such ordination, which immediately qualified them for all ministerial work. But in the setting apart of these two apostles, there is no record indicating that any virtue was imparted by the mere act of laying on of hands."[119]

It must be stated here that although the church found it necessary to certify workers in the late 1800s, biblical ordination existed long before. Further clarity was sought as to the gender of ordinands. In other words, the criterion above was based on preferred characteristics of which gender was not stipulated and most certainly, the question must have been asked if females could be included. Here is the clarification to such a question in the second resolution:

Two further resolutions went the *General Conference in 1881 and 1888 read:*

1.   *Resolved: That all candidates for license and ordination*

[119] Ellen Gould White, Acts of the Apostles, p. 162. Review and Herald Publishing Association, Washington, DC. 1974.

should be examined with reference to their intellectual and spiritual fitness for the successful discharge of the duties which will devolve upon them as licentiates and ordained ministers.

2.   Resolved: That females possessing the necessary qualifications to fill that position, may, with perfect propriety, be set apart by ordination to the work of the Christian ministry.[120]

We have a record of the first resolution being adopted but not the second, if not why? Based on the reason for ordination and the criteria set, it made perfect sense with a female heading the organisation as a prophetess to have her included.

Ellen G. White, considered as one demonstrating the call to the prophetic ministry, supported the resolutions above. The following statement appears to be a strong rebuttal to the question about a female's illegibility, **"This question is not for men to settle. The Lord has settled it. You are to do your duty to the women who labor in the gospel".** The Lord she said has settled it, it was not just her opinion, it was God's. She emphasised that "they", whoever they were, should "do their duty to women".

Seven years later she penned the following statement published in 1895:

> "Women who are willing to consecrate some of their time to the service of the Lord should be appointed to visit the sick, look after the young, and minister to the necessities of the poor. They should be set apart for this work by prayer and laying on of hands. In some cases, they will need to counsel with the church officers or the minister; but if they are devoted women, maintaining a vital connection with God, they will be a power for good in the church. This is another means of strengthening and building up the church. We need to branch out more in our methods of labour. Not a hand should be bound, not a soul discouraged, **not a voice should be hushed; let every individual labour, privately or publicly,** to

---

[120] http://www.adventistarchives.org/docs/GCB/GCB1863-88. pdf#view=fit) (Accessed August, 23, 2016).

help forward this grand work, **place the burdens upon men and women of the church**, that they may grow by reason of the exercise, and thus become effective agents in the hand of the Lord for the enlightenment of those who sit in darkness.[121] *This could not be clearer, women should not be silenced, they should be engaged in private and public ministry and should carry, "The burdens", responsibility or leadership positions. Could the church begin to pick and choose what it wants when the Lord has spoken?*

According to the White Estate, "There is no record of Ellen G. White ever having been ordained by the laying on of human hands. {No fault of hers. Her counsel above says that those who do the ministry of Christ should be set apart}. Yet from 1871 until her death, she was granted "ministerial credentials" by various organisations of the church. The certificate that was used said, "Ordained Minister." Three of her credential certificates from the mid-1880s are still in our possession. It is interesting to note that on one of them (1885) the word "ordained" is neatly struck out. On the 1887 certificate, the next one we have, it is not."[122]

Ellen G. White, referring in 1911 to her own call to service, wrote the following: **"In the city of Portland the Lord ordained me as His messenger,** and here my first labours were given to the cause of present truth"[123] Sound very much like the Apostle Paul who said, "But when it pleased God, who separated me from my mother's womb and called *me* by his grace." Galatians 1:15 or Like Jeremiah of whom it was said that the Lord ordained him. "Before I formed you in the womb, I knew you; before you were born, I sanctified you; I ordained you a

---

[121] E. G. White, Review and Herald, July 9, (1895). https://m.egwwritings.org/en/book/83.339#343. (Accessed February 12, 2022).

[122] https://whiteestate.org/legacy/issues-egw_credentials-egw_credentials-htm/. Compiled by the Ellen G. White Estate, Inc. (2018). (Accessed August 20, 2016).

[123] E. G. White Writings, Letters and Manuscripts Volume 24 (1909) p. 5 https://m.egwwritings.org/en/book/14074.9828001#9828012. (Accessed July 10, 2019).

prophet to the nations." Jeremiah 1:5.

What the church did or did not do to Ellen G. White is not the test of truth or biblical teaching. "And the times of this ignorance God winked at; but now commandeth all men everywhere to repent:" Acts 17:30. In ignorance, we do many things and make many mistakes, "But the path of the just is as the shining light, that shineth more and more unto the perfect day". Proverbs 4:18. Now we know better, now we see clearly through the light of God's word, therefore, we do well to auger our teachings as directed from scripture and not from tradition or culture.

Ellen G. White urged **"Women to help carry the truth— God wants workers who can carry the truth to all classes, high and low, rich and poor. In this work, women may act an important part. God grant that those who read these words may put forth earnest efforts to present an open door for consecrated women to enter the field."**[124] A clear appeal to the men or women in leadership, not to block the path or frustrate the will of God by excluding women form being set apart.

"The Effectiveness of Women's Work. Women can be the instruments of righteousness, rendering holy service. It was Mary that first preached about a risen Jesus... If there were twenty women where now there is one, who would make this holy mission their cherished work, we should see many more converted to the truth. The refining, softening influence of Christian women is needed in the great work of preaching the truth". — The Review and Herald, January 2, 1879.

The White Estate adds:

"Several women were ordained as deaconesses during Ellen White's Australian ministry. On August 10, 1895, the nominating committee at the Ashfield church in Sydney rendered its report, which was approved. The clerk's minutes for that date state: 'Immediately following the election, the officers were called to the front where Pastors Corliss and McCullagh set apart

---

[124] 111   E. G. White, Manuscript Releases 5:162, https://m. egwwritings.org/en/book/83.339#343. (Accessed October 10, 2022).

the elder, deacons, [and] deaconesses by prayer and the laying on of hands.' Several years later, in the same church, W. C. White officiated at the ordination of the church officers.

The minutes of the Ashfield church for January 7, 1900, state: 'The previous Sabbath officers had been nominated and accepted for the current year, and today Elder White ordained and laid hands on the elders, deacon, and deaconesses."[125] Yes, the Whites supported women being ordained or more accurately, set apart.

Ellen G. White further makes the case for parity for women:

"There are women who should labour in the gospel ministry. In many respects, they would do more good than the ministers who neglect to visit the flock of God...This question is not for men to settle. The Lord has settled it. You are to do your duty to the women who labour in the gospel, whose work testifies that they are essential to carry the truth into families. Their work is just the work that must be done. In many respects, a woman can impart knowledge to her sisters that a man cannot. The cause would suffer great loss without this kind of labour"[126]. "Women who do such labour, especially full time, were to be paid fairly for their work from the tithe. The tithe should go to those who labour in word and doctrine, be they men, or women." She added, "Seventh-day Adventists are not in any way to belittle woman's work."[127]

The Bible does not forbid women to speak or exercise authority. We see this fact upheld by many scriptures, beginning with Deborah who was a prophet and judge in Israel and nine other female prophets in the Bible. I call upon the Seventh-day Adventist Church to at least be consistent because there has been

[125] The Review and Herald, (1895).
https://m.egwwritings.org/en/book/821.14323#14323. (Accessed February 20, 2016).
[126] Manuscript Release. https://m.egwwritings.org/en/ book/56.1578#1589. (Accessed February 20, 2016).
[127] Ibid. Manuscript Release.
https://egwwritings.org/en/book/56.1578#1589. (Accessed February 20, 2016).

no greater authority given to anyone in the denomination than that of Ellen G. White who spoke and led the church from its inception, and whose voice is authoritative today. Was Ellen G. White not called and ordained by God for this purpose? Did she not occupy a position of authority? Outside of the Bible, the inspired writings of Ellen G. White, though they do not replace the Bible or equate to the Bible, remain the most authoritative source of information after the Bible, in the SDA Church.

Mrs White's prolific and inspired commentaries, counsels, admonitions and letters still serve authoritatively and are owned by what is known as the White Estate. How can the SDA church in the same breath disallow women their full voice and vocational opportunities when it's most authoritative figure and voice is a female who pleaded with them to accept the counsels from the Lord concerning women? 1 Thessalonians 5:19, 20 "Do not quench the Spirit. **Do not despise** prophesying". The church is guilty of despising prophesying by not applying the clear instructions given by the Bible and Mrs White.

If St. Paul meant literally that women should not speak and exercise authority, did Mrs White's role contradict Paul's injunctions? Are we being consistent in our interpretation and application of the scriptures? If, in our tradition, a woman rose to such a level of authority, why is the church, in the same breath withholding the credentials of women? Or at worst, splitting hairs with a different name to mark a woman's call to ministry (Commissioning for women and ordination for men)? Is the church intentionally denying the gift of the Holy Spirit which Joel declared would be poured out upon "All flesh", specifying "Men and women" and "Maidens"? "Surely the Lord God will do nothing, but he revealeth his secret unto his servants the prophets." Amos 3:7. The church is not without prophetic guidance, it must not "Despise prophesying" 1 Thessalonians 5:20

The General Conference of Seventh-day Adventists has developed a global initiative in response to ending violence against women, men and children called "enditnow". According to their vision, "enditnow is the most important stand the

Seventh-day Adventist Church has ever taken regarding violence against men, women and children."[128] Enditnow's web page acknowledges, "Although it is an uncomfortable subject for many people, it has become more and more obvious that abuse is a serious problem for Christians and Seventh-day Adventists. **Abuse in any form deforms the body of Christ".[129] A VERY FRANK ACKNOWLEDGEMENT INDEED!**

Two of the five enditnow's strategic objectives are to:

1. **"Examine church policies and practices to be sure none foster or encourage hurtful or discriminatory attitudes towards women, children, or men."**

2. **"Help raise awareness. Share materials about gender-based violence with your community."**

This book *Justice for Women: The Cry to End the Pandemic of Discrimination, Intimidation, Misogyny, Abuse and Violence against Women in Society and Religious Communities* does just that, it helps to raise awareness and provide materials about the thinking and justification that undergirds gender-based violence. It also examines the church's policies and practices which foster and encourage hurtful and discriminatory attitudes toward women. The theology of women and ordination as presented from the Bible in this book renders the church's teaching and policies on women in breach of its own enditnow policy.

My hunch is that in many parts of the world where people do not accept or subscribe to ontological or functional equality, it's because the Christian Church for many years portrayed women as being less than equal to men. In other words, the misinterpretation of scripture has led to a global culture of patriarchy, misogyny, and discrimination against women.

Even if the Church was to make an edict or declaration to end

---

[128] https://www.enditnow.org/?_
ga=2.70805456.1741611856.1661869720946674805.1661869720.
(Accessed October 26,2020).
[129] Ibid.

inequality, today, it will take decades for functional equality to be inculcated at all levels of society. We cannot afford to delay any longer to make this declaration. The Church must not keep silent and allow culture to undermine scripture. Unity or coercion at the expense of truth and fairness is injustice. Culture is not above scripture and conformity is not unity. The book Justice for Women is a call for the church to be united around scripture and not divided by culture: a call for religious communities to be silent no more on the call for Justice for women.

Where culture clashes with the scripture, churches should mitigate them through education and dialogue, not silence or compromise. Where there are no such difficulties, churches should practice the word of God and promote functional equality in the body of Christ. By admission, the SDA church acknowledges that the equality of women is not a theological issue but a sociological one. It's affirmation of women is congruent with the ordination of women.

I call upon faith leaders and communities to:

1.   Be consistent, not just to put nice sounding words on paper, but to implement policies of equal opportunity as above: "Examine church policies and practices to be sure none fosters or encourage hurtful or discriminatory attitudes towards women, children, or men."

2.   Have the courage to acknowledge the failure of the church to treat women equally and "Help raise awareness. Share materials about {gender-bias and its relationship to} gender-based violence with your community." (Words in parenthesis supplied by author)

3.   Adopt the inspired, well thought through and worded resolution of 1888 which reads: *"Resolved: That females possessing the necessary qualifications to fill that position, may, with perfect propriety, be set apart by ordination to the work of the Christian ministry.*[130]

4.   *Use gender-inclusive language in ordination policies. Change the references to the ordinant as a "he" to the one, the*

---

[130] (http://www.adventistarchives.org/docs/GCB/GCB1863-88.pdf#view=fit) (Accessed August, 23, 2016).

person or the candidate.

5.   *Repent of the sins of patriarchy and inequality and apologise to women.*

6.   *Trust God for the consequences of speaking the truth in the face of cultural norms and expectations. The church must not afford unity at the expense of suppressing the truth and discriminating against others.*

7.   *To respect the Protected Characteristics enshrined in law (European, British and American) for a person's right to be free from discrimination of race, religion, gender or age etc.*

Where do we stand today?

Let not the church complicate what the spirit has simplified.
Let's be biblical:

1.   God calls and ordains. Jeremiah 1:5
2.   God calls regardless of gender. Joel 2:28.
3.   The Holy Spirit calls and gifts whomsoever he wills. 1 Corinthians 12:1-12.
4.   Jesus chose and ordained disciples (those who obey him, not a specific gender) Jn 15;16. Twelve males were not prescriptive but descriptive.
5.   St. Paul said that markers of race, ethnicity, class and gender are non-starters in the church. Galatians 3:28.

If the Holy Spirit so wills should the church question it?

Ordination is God's foreknowledge at work in choosing us to be part of his plan, even before we were conceived. The first step toward ordination is initiated by God. God breathes on anything that will be accepted and used by him. Therefore, a theology of ordination begins with the recognition that the Holy Spirit is already at work in the believer's life. This is evident by conversion and the spiritual gifts or fruits manifested. The very important second step is the role of the church in the process, a local group or congregation endorses what God has already birthed and made manifest, i.e., the gift of leadership, singing, exhortation, preaching etc., in a believer,

be they male or female. The first step can be classified as qualification, (The work of the Holy Spirit) and the second, confirmation, (The work of the church).

Having surveyed both the Old and the New Testaments, we have not seen any justification for the exclusion of women in the plan of God. On the contrary, we have seen the Holy Spirit empowering women to be God's mouthpieces and ambassadors in the history of Israel, the New Testament Church and definitely throughout the history of the Christian Church, and today, as prophesied in Joel 2:28.

The New Testament concept of the church is as the human body with many different parts; none more important than the other, a kingdom of priests, 1 Peter 2:4-9. The Bible teaches about the priesthood of all believers. According to St. Paul in First Corinthians, within the fellowship of the kingdom of Christ, race, social status and gender cannot be factors to credit or discredit a believer from serving or ministering. Galatians 3:28.

Deborah's story in the Old Testament informs the thinking as to the role of women as leaders in the church; it may well be one of the narratives about women in the scriptures that answers the questions as to whether a woman should speak and exercise authority? Are we doing justice to the scriptures and to the Apostle Paul if on one hand, we quote that women should be silent and not teach or exercise authority, but still practice otherwise? Do the narratives of women confirm or deny that a woman should be silent and subordinate? Joel 2:28 confirmed that God pours out his spirit on males and females without distinction, what is the church's biblical basis for speaking contrarily? Should women be allowed equal access to all leadership roles in the church as their male counterparts? If we determine our practices in the light of the scriptures and not culture, the answer would be a resounding, yes.

The New Testament concept of the church is not a hierarchical structure but a level playing field where all are invited to follow Jesus, and all are commissioned to go and make disciples. Where, then is the biblical justification for refusing

to endorse women who are equally called and set apart by the Holy Spirit?

I put it to you that the Protestant view and understanding of the church as Laos, poses no contradiction for women and men to be equally included in the leadership of the church. The biblical understanding of spiritual gifts makes room for females to be set apart for ministry in whatever sphere their gifts make room for them. The church recognises the working of the Holy Spirit upon new believers as the greatest endorsement one could have. The church does not initiate the calling but acknowledges it. It is in this context that the term ordination has specific significance. "Evangelicals and Protestants view the church as a community of reconciled sinners; a kingdom of priests and not a dispenser of divine grace."[131]

The Church's working policy should protect and be inclusive of all. We cannot discriminate against women of God, in the name of God, in the house of God. A gender-inclusive church policy would make ordination certification available to all its members including women. We cannot on one hand ordain female deacons and elders but deny female ministers' ordination, or at worst, ordain men and not women, giving a different name to the service for recognition of females, this anomaly has no scriptural basis.

In the time of ignorance, God winks, but now he commanded all men to repent. I call on leaders to stand up and be counted, to take the side of scripture and not culture regarding treating women equally.

Churches and other religious communities should take the lead in washing their hands from the sin of patriarchy, misogyny, abuse and discrimination against the fairer sex. They must promote the equality of human beings and stop the discrimination against women which leads to other forms of

---

[131] Pierce, Ronald W. Groothuis, Rebecca Merrill Fee, Gordon D. p. 277.

abuse. The Christian Church's failure to "Rightly divide the word of truth" has led to institutional discrimination against women. The use of the Bible authoritatively to justify a less-than-equal place for women has contributed to the way women have been seen and treated over the centuries. The Church cannot conscientiously call for an end to the abuse of women without examining its interpretation of scripture upon which the foundation of patriarchy, misogyny, inequality and discrimination against women have been predicated.

Churches must set the moral compass for society. It must declare what is right and wrong, what's ethical and unethical. It must indeed call out discrimination as sinful in the sight of God. Failure to do so is an injustice to society and a serious affront to God. Abuse and discrimination of women in any form, which is far too prevalent in society, must not be swept under the carpet or flooring in the house of God; by men of God; to children of God or tolerated in society.

There are a few countries in our world that have made laws to protect women from systemic, corporate and domestic abuse and discrimination, I applaud them. Some religious institutions and businesses have instituted policies to guarantee equality for women, and I applaud them, also.

Religious institutions should not be last to cry out against the discrimination of women and girls, or anyone for that matter. The prophet Amos said, "But let **justice** roll out like waters, And **righteousness** like an ever-flowing stream". Amos 5:24. The prophet Isaiah said, "Cry aloud and spare not", Isaiah 58:1. Jesus himself said, "The Spirit of the Lord is upon me because he hath anointed me to preach the gospel to the poor; he hath sent me to heal the broken-hearted, to preach deliverance to the captives, and recovering of sight to the blind, to set at liberty them that are bruised". Luke 4:18. Yes, majority of religious devotees are women and they are bruised and hurting, they need the gospel which liberates and heals. Justice is righteousness right doing.

Churches are mandated to lift their voice to end the pandemic of discrimination and abuse against women, especially women and girls who are the victims of domestic and institutionalised discrimination and abuse. Far too many women have had to endure abuse from men. Male harassment and abuse are too prevalent and painful. Women should not pay such a high price for simply being in a female body.

Men can be protectors, not predators; lovers, not abusers; providers, not users; liberators and not enslavers. Imagine with me, a world where women are given their rightful Value, Visibility, Voice, and Vocational opportunities. Imagine a society, organisations, businesses, churches, temples, mosques, communities and families, where women are treated equally, fairly, respected, and valued. Imagine a world where girls and women feel safe to enjoy their femininity and not become victims of crime, violence, abuse or discrimination. I call upon men, especially those in positions of influence to help us realise this world.

In the words of Karen Holford, "Let's make our world a better place for women and everyone else". "Yes we can"[132]

---

[132] Barak Obama's speech to supporters after losing the New Hampshire's Democratic primary to Hilary Clinton on 8 January 2008. NPR. https://www.npr.org/2008/11/05/96624326/transcript-of-barack-obamas-victory-speech. (Accessed June 7, 2023).

Chapter 6
Summary

"There's a long, long history of women suffering abuse, injustice, and not having the same opportunities as men, and I think that's been very detrimental to the human race as a whole."

—*Joseph Gordon-Levitt, American actor*

Synopsis

I cannot imagine a world without women in it, and neither could God. Every man, woman, boy and girl who entered this world came through a woman. According to the Genesis account of creation, the woman is God's crowning act in creation. On the 6th day of creation, when God had created everything including man, God saw that the world was incomplete (the woman was not yet created), so God created woman, the part of God himself that reflects wisdom, beauty, desire, intuition, endurance, nurture and strength-Woman. That should make us all smile.

The woman was indispensable in God's creative plans for the universe. If the infinite God felt that there was no other way to bring completion to the universe than by crowning his works with the creation of Eve, it means that women are infinitely valuable and indispensable in the eyes of an infinite God! That deserves a wow! God needed a woman on board for his universe to function, and a woman made in his image: possessing the characteristics of the Godhead, love, oneness and equality. Male and female are God's patent. We want our women to rise, for there is life after discrimination and abuse. We want all females to realise their God-given potential. Real men will give agency to realising a fairer and safer world for the women and girls in it.

We cannot escape the evidence that, to a large degree, discrimination against women has been influenced by the theology of religious institutions and their interpretation or, more accurately, their misinterpretation of specific sacred texts. Sacred texts were taken from their '*Sitz im Leben*' or life setting and applied literally and universally. In other words, Bible interpreters applied poor exegetical and hermeneutical skills. For centuries, even millennia, the Church's interpretation of a few passages of the scriptures has led to a theology about women that distorts, demeans, demoralises, and discriminates against women.

The influence of Christianity on society in the main has been

a positive one, however, its theology on women has impacted women negatively. Its theology has limited and excluded women from equal standing and opportunity as human beings, often defended on ontological, soteriological and cultural grounds.

We began by acknowledging the sensitivities surrounding the issues of women's roles, and I would like to conclude on the same note by recognising these sensitivities in various cultures and traditions worldwide. This book traced and refuted society's arguments and justification for patriarchy, male privilege, misogyny and the systemic limitation of women which has contributed to the mindset that discriminates against women globally.

There are three key presuppositions about women that are at the heart of misogyny, patriarchy, gender privilege, and discrimination against women:

1. The superiority of males over females. That the creation narrative of a man being created first and a woman second as a helpmeet, gives males an ontological advantage over females.

2. That the woman's seduction by the serpent and the ensuing consequence for her role in the entrance of sin into the world, relegated all women to a position of perpetual subordination, submission, and silence.

3. The patriarchal interpretation of the Apostle Paul's injunctions about women. That the Bible provides the rationale for the limitation of women.

Equality from the beginning

The Genesis account of the world's creation facilitates a theological understanding of human relationships and the relationship of humans to their environment as declared by the One called the Creator.

The Genesis account refutes the widely held presuppositions of inequality between males and females and the limitation of females, or their relegation to roles of submission, subordination and silence by establishing:

1. **Mutual ontology or being; "in the image of God created he them, male and female created he them" Gen1:27. The image and likeness of God is comprised of love, oneness, unity, and equality, these characteristics were resident in both male and female. NO HIERARCHY IN THE TRINITY. Simply put, Adam and Eve were created as equals.**

2. **Mutual dominion: That Adam and Eve were both assigned dominion "let them have dominion over the earth" Gen1:28. Dominion is authority. Both Adam and Eve were given authority over creation and not dominion or domination over each other.**

3. **Mutual culpability & punishment: regarding the entrance of sin into the world, both Adam and Eve were held accountable and with equity, both suffered the consequences. Woman's assignment of dominion did not change after the fall, "He shall rule over thee" meant that AS A WIFE, her independence would become interdependence, meaning that Adam would become Eve's accountability partner. Eve must not work independently of Adam but mutually.**

4. **Mutual redemption from the fall. That both Adam and Eve were saved by the same sacrifice...that there was no gender distinction in their salvation.**

Sin did not reverse the equality or nature of Adam or Eve, neither did it change their status to have dominion or authority.

1. Adam and Eve possessed equally, all the characteristics which constitute the image and likeness of Father, Son and Holy Spirit: love, unity and equality. Both man and woman were created in the image of God in which there is no hierarchy. Man was not created ontologically superior to woman, neither was the woman demoted or sentenced punitively as often caricatured, for the entrance of sin into the world. We can be grateful for the first three chapters of Genesis, which, to a great extent, set out a theology of gender which adequately describes the nature or ontology, status and roles of both man and woman with mutuality. After the fall, a promise (Genesis 3:15) was made to both, that God will intervene to crush the cause of the hatred, indifference, discord, domination and inequality that would have developed because of man's transgression.

2. The argument of Adam being created first (pre-eminence-first in time) as an ontological or natural advantage over Eve, is a myth. First does not mean superior; it simply has to do with the arrangement of time and order, not quality. If 5 cars came off the production line; the first was red, the second was blue, and the third orange, are we to assume that the first or red car was superior to the blue car because it was the first? That's preposterous. Likewise, it is preposterous to infer or even state that Adam had some ontological advantage over Eve simply because he was created first. First, the creation order is not a statement of value or worth.

Helpmeet, meaning: Genesis 2:18 states, "*And the LORD God said, It is not good that the man should be alone; I will make him a helpmeet for him.*" The designation of the woman as a helpmeet to the man in Genesis chapter 2 is of primary interest to the discussion about the role of women. The traditional reading of "Helpmeet" connotes someone who is in a subordinate position: someone who just assists. On the contrary, the Hebrew word "Ezer" for "Helpmeet", clarifies any ambiguity about the role of a woman; it means, "One who is the same as the other and who

172

surrounds, protects, aids, helps, supports." The word *Ezer* in the scripture is otherwise used only of God as our helper.

"When God decided to assuage the loneliness of Adam by creating for him a "helpmeet", God did not give Adam someone inferior to him to help him out. This line of reasoning is not supported in the text, rather; God gave someone equal to Adam, as the solution to his loneliness."[133]

E.G. White says, "Eve was created from a rib taken from the side of Adam, signifying that she was not to control him as the head, nor to be trampled under his feet as an inferior, but to stand by his side as an equal, to be loved and protected by him."[134]

Adam and Eve's relationship represented the love, oneness, unity, and equality in their maker. "A hierarchical order was not conceived in God's mind, nor expressed in their relationship with each other; therefore, a hierarchical relationship between Adam and Eve would not have reflected the image and likeness of God."[135]

Sin, silence, submission and subordination

Women have been blamed for the entrance of sin into the world and subsequently seem to be under the sentence of subordination to men for their role in the original sin. Evidently, subordination is not substantiated in the Genesis account. The penalty for the fall was conferred on both Eve and Adam. Genesis 3:16, 17 reads: "Unto the woman he said, I will greatly multiply thy sorrow and thy conception; in sorrow, thou shalt bring forth children; and thy desire shall be to thy husband, and he shall rule over thee.

---

[133] Pierce, Ronald W. Groothuis, Rebecca Merrill Fee, Gordon D. Discovering Biblical Equality: Complementarity Without Hierarchy (Downers Grove, IL, InterVarsity Press, 2005), p. 86.
[134] Ellen G. White, Evangelism (Washington, D.C., 1946), p.472.
[135] Pierce, Ronald W. Groothuis, Rebecca Merrill Fee, Gordon D. pp. 84-85.

And unto Adam, he said, because, thou hast hearkened unto the voice of thy wife, and hast eaten of the tree, of which I commanded thee, saying, thou shalt not eat of it: cursed is the ground for thy sake; in sorrow shalt thou eat of it all the days of thy life." Wouldn't God be punitive to punish Eve more than Adam? Shouldn't it be the other way around where Adam should receive the greater punishment because 1 Timothy 2:14 says that Eve was deceived but Adam was not because he consciously made that wrong decision? God jointly held the two responsible, there was parity in God's discipline.

"He shall rule over thee"

To rule also connotes measurement, a fixed arrangement. Eve and Adam must consult together, she must not now go it alone. (That's how Eve was tempted). As the sun rules the day and the moon rules the night, Adam was to give light to Eve's decisions, in other words, "Adam would be Eve's accountability partner." The statement "He shall rule over thee" was more descriptive rather than prescriptive. Remember, dominion as in rule or control was given to both Adam and Eve over creation and not over each other. There is no explicit reversal of the dominion given them. Even in the world of nature, sin had devastating effects on things animate and inanimate. We are still experiencing the ecological fallouts today, but these were not prescribed but described. God did not prescribed laws to destroy the earth but described the consequences or fall-out of sin.

A theological understanding of these issues is foundational for interpreting other passages of the scriptures which, on the surface, may seem to suggest otherwise. **Therefore, we leave the Genesis account without any ambiguity about the nature and role of the woman; created in the image and likeness of God, as was man; given dominion over the earth, as was the man; equally held responsible for the entrance of sin, as was man, and equally punished and forgiven, as was the man**.

More than housewives, seductresses and temptresses

Women in the Old Testament were called and gifted; they occupied positions of authority alongside men. From prophetesses and judges to queens, the stories of women in the Old Testament, far from painting a picture of silence and subordination, place women in positions of authority and ability accompanied by great feats that have been unparalleled. The stories of women in the Old Testament also portray a far nobler picture of women than being temptresses, seductresses and subordinates, or remaining within a fixed role as a housewife. In Proverbs chapter 31, Lemuel's mother tells him about the awesome characteristics of a woman in a beautiful acrostic. The fairer sex is described as an individual who is industrious, intuitive, insightful, intelligent, indefatigable, irreplaceable and irresistible, yes, someone who is ambidextrous, versatile, and priceless!

Jesus and real men make room for women's gifts.

In the time of Jesus, women were forbidden to speak publicly to a male. Women were not considered credible as a witness. Witnesses were commonly used in everyday life but according to Jewish convention, female witnesses were on the list of persons who were not competent to testify. The Talmud suggested that a woman's place was in the home and that a man was not allowed to speak to a woman in public. Against this backdrop, we can better appreciate Jesus's interaction with women.

Jesus's first post-resurrection appearance was to a woman. Not to angels, apostles, faithful Joseph, or the true-hearted Nicodemus, but a woman! Mary was not the noblest of women either, i.e., his mother or Anna; Mary was the one out of whom he cast seven devils! *"Now when Jesus was risen early the first day of the week, he appeared first to Mary Magdalene, out of whom he had cast seven devils."* Mark 16:9. The Angel's conversation with Mary in Mark 16:7, 10, is interesting, *"But go, tell his disciples and Peter, 'He is going ahead of you into Galilee. There you will see him, just as he told you.'" "She went and told them that had been with him, as they mourned and wept."* Verse 11 continues – **"And they, when they heard that he was alive, and had seen of her, disbelieved."** *Note the phrase, "and had been seen of her" because women were not considered as a witness!*

Wow! A woman as a witness? Why would Jesus risk commissioning this incredible story to a woman? And of all women, one who once had a questionable background? **What a paradox! In a society where women were forbidden to be witnesses, we see Jesus intentionally making a point by appearing first to a woman and putting her in a situation contrary to the conventions of his day. Jesus elevated women and gave them back their voices. Women were among the very first to be commissioned, to go tell. Jesus never silenced women. He empowered them. The Church will do well to follow Jesus.**

Was St. Paul a misogynist?

Did he overrule Jesus? Definitely not. Well, what did Paul mean when he said that women should not speak or exercise authority?

Against the backdrop of the Old Testament and Jesus's radical affirmation of women giving them Value, Visibility, and Voice, why would St Paul want to run into conflict, contradict the scriptures and at worst, contradict himself? Because the scriptures are a coherent whole and all are inspired, we must harmonise what various authors have said and not put one author against another, or even worst, put an author against himself. Even when it appears that two authors are saying something different, we have to assume that this discrepancy is highly impossible because God inspired all the scriptures.

Diligent bible study, proper exegesis and hermeneutics help

harmonise what the scripture teaches. We have acknowledged that this does require some in-depth analysis at times, an appreciation for the different genres of the scriptures and an understanding of their '*Sitz im Leben*'. There are many teachings embedded in the scriptures that are not discernible if unsearched. Jesus taught many truths in parables which were not understood by surface reading or listening, such was the case with the narratives about women, they contain the key to unlock a theology about women that empowers women and not limit them. That's why we are admonished to "study" (do exegesis the theological discipline of searching out or drawing out what Bible authors said in their context or *Sitz im Leben*-life setting) and "Rightly divide the word of truth" (hermeneutics the theological discipline of interpreting the scriptures). We've concluded that the issue with the Apostle Paul's prohibitions about women is a hermeneutical problem, one of interpretation that involves proper exegesis and careful study of his sayings in relation to their context and the rest of the scriptures.

The Apostle Paul was not a misogynist. Rather than limiting women's voices and authority, he affirmed them. While paying due regard to Roman law, forbidding women to speak publicly, h e was unequivocal about women being discriminated against because of their gender. He was explicit about women's full participation in the church by recognising the gifts of the Holy Spirit given to males and females alike as was prophesied by the prophet Joel. St. Paul commended female deacons and women who were praying and prophesying publicly. **"But every woman that prays or prophesies with *her* head uncovered dishonours her head: for that is even all one as if she were shaven." (1 Corinthians 11:5) Paul spoke of women who laboured with him in ministry, "And I entreat thee also, true yoke fellow, help those women which laboured with me in the gospel" (Philippians 4:3.) Clearly, Paul wrote Letters of Occasion, what applied to one church or context did not apply to all others. He actually preserved the credibility of the scriptures by writing various letters, rather than sending the same letter around to all the churches, which would have been chaos.** His most robust defence for women's full participation and equality was in the following words. "There is neither Jew nor Greek; there is neither bond nor free, there is neither male nor female: for ye are all one in Christ Jesus." Galatians 3:28 The Apostle Paul acknowledged that distinctions of race, nationality and gender exist in the world, but it should not be so in the body of Christ.

Ordination: (As one without authority): Gendered privileges and spaces.

Ordination: "Then the word of the Lord came unto me, saying, Before *I formed thee* in the belly *I knew thee*, and before thou camest forth out of the womb *I sanctified thee*, and *I ordained thee* a prophet unto the nations." (Jeremiah 1:5). God, the Holy Spirit, is the one who does the ordaining or setting aside, not a creed or a need but the sovereign will and foreknowledge of God who predestines whomsoever they will fulfil their purpose. The genesis of ordination existed long before churches established their reasons to practice ordination. Ordination is not a sacrament the church grants to a worthy qualifier based on class, race, education, gender or the like. It is not a human phenomenon that one mortal confers upon another; it is what God initiated long before the ordinant themself came into existence and began participating in God's divine and sovereign will.

Ordination is God's foreknowledge at work in choosing us to be part of his plan, even before we were conceived. The church simply presides over the realisation of God's calling in the life of one called by God.

The calling of mankind to repentance, their conversion, subsequent giftedness and commission to go into the world is initiated by the Holy Spirit without regard to gender. 1 Corinthians 12:11 makes it clear that the same Spirit is at work in all these things, distributing to each person as he chooses. The Church's only part in the ordination process is giving ascent to what the Spirit already has done. In the Apostolic age, there is no trace of the doctrine of an outward rite conferring inward grace. However, we have instances of the formal appointment or recognition of those who had already given proof of their spiritual qualification.

Women's gifts make room for their ordination, not the other way around, where their ordination will determine their gifts or ministry. To deny women their God-given Value, Visibility, Voice, and Vocation because they are female is to be branded patriarchal, discriminatory and misogynistic. Instead, let's empower women as our Creator, Jesus and Apostle Paul did, liberating them from centuries of subjugation by acknowledging their God-given Value, Visibility, Voice and Vocation.

The Church cannot use ordination as a gender-based ordinance. We are very clear that the gifts of God and the calling of God are without regard to gender. In both the Old and New Testaments, we have seen women who were called by God's Spirit, gifted and commissioned by him to affect his purposes. Therefore, there is no biblical or theological basis for excluding women from being ordained. Ordination is not a man-made ordinance of the church. Once the Church recognises the work of the Holy Spirit in the life of a believer through their giftedness or when a missional need has been identified and persons deployed to fill that need, then the criterion for the manmade ceremony we term ordination or laying on of hands would have been met. It will be entirely sexist and misogynistic to exclude anyone who has met the criterion. After all, Joel 2:28 endorses the Holy Spirit's manifestation in the lives of females in the Old Testament and the last days.

Churches should be consistent in their theology. Some churches would not ordain a female at all, others ordain female deacons and elders but not ministers. Ordination when applied theologically should include all elected church officers, regardless of gender. There is no varying type of ordination based on the responsibility given or on gender characteristics; ordination is ordination.

Theologically speaking, if we recognise the gifts given by God to a believer, then we have identified the calling of God on that person's life or their ordination. Then, the church is invited and obligated to officially give its endorsement or acknowledgement, by appointing the one ordained by God.

Who then will be the voice to speak up for the large group of women in society, our churches and religious institutions to be included and not excluded; to be counted in and not counted out? Jesus gave women Value, Visibility, and Voice; the churches and other faith groups today must do no different. May God grant us the courage to break into our culture and traditions with the principles of God's kingdom and make the necessary changes; to be consistent in standing on the side of scripture and not culture. Let's allow the Holy Spirit to move and not stand in the way.

Jesus fought for a just society. If He were here today, He definitely would be on the climate agenda, but equally so, on the justice agenda for equal social participation and treatment of women. He would be a voice to empower women. However, in Jesus's place, the Church is the custodian of His word and must be his voice for gender equality. Jesus replaced the partition wall between the various social groups; therefore, there should be no qualitative difference between Jew and Gentile, Black and White, male and female. These distinctions society makes to define us, actually divide us. These markers must not exist in the kingdom of God. Jesus prayed "That they all may be one; as thou, Father, art in me, and I in thee, that they also may be one in us: that the world may believe that thou hast sent me." (John 17:21). Jesus becomes the new hermeneutic of both Old and New Testaments, what he said and did supersede all other prophets (Hebrews 1:1). "Search the scriptures; for in them ye think ye have eternal life: and they are they which testify of me." Every scripture finds its fulfilment in Jesus. In other words, we can simply ask in every situation of doubt, 'What would Jesus do'?

If God so created woman, saved, called, and commissioned her, as in the examples of Jesus, what authority has the church to disregard, demean, devalue and discriminate against women? The foundation on which the church has

built its edifice on a limited role for women is discriminatory.

In British law, there are protected characteristics. "It is against the law to discriminate against someone because of:

- age
- disability
- gender reassignment
- marriage and civil partnership
- pregnancy and maternity
- race
- religion or belief
- sex
- sexual orientation. "[136]

These are called protected characteristics and the Church must be compliant. Think for a moment, what would it feel like to be discriminated against because of your age, disability, gender, race or religion? The golden rule says, "As you would that men do to you, do ye likewise unto them". If we were to practice the golden rule, most of our interpersonal issues would not even surface. The word of God requires us to treat each other without partiality and it sets the standard for justice, "He hath shewed thee, O man, what is good; and what doth the LORD require of thee, but to **do justly**, and to love mercy, and to walk humbly with thy God." Micah 6:8. The Bible is the standard of truth and doctrine, and it does not fail to hold the Church accountable for justice.

"Let **justice** roll out like waters, And righteousness like an ever-flowing stream. Amos 5:24

---

[136] https://www.equalityhumanrights.com/en/equality-act/protected-characteristics. (Accessed 30, October, 2022).

Reversing the pandemic of discrimination

Inadvertently, the Protestant and Roman Catholic Churches contributed to the widespread discrimination of women due to their interpretation of the scriptures. These Churches must now seize every opportunity to defend the dignity and equality of all human beings and wash their hands of the sins of patriarchy and misogyny. Jesus is the head of the church; he made women in his image. To hurt women is to hurt the head of the church, Christ himself. The ill-treatment of women for centuries is a sin in God's sight and a hindrance to the progress and witness of the church. It is time for a climate change in our world for women.

Yes, there are many challenges our world face post pandemic: climate and ecological issues, Transgenderism, LGBTQIA+, inflation, scarcity, mental health, immigration and the threat of artificial intelligence (AI), however, as we navigate these realities, the Christian Church must:

- Practice zero tolerance for bullying, harassment, intimidation, exploitation, violation and discrimination of women.
- Protect victims, and prosecute predators.
- Apologize to women globally for the sins of patriarchy, misogyny and male privilege, perpetuated through the misinterpretation and application of the scriptures.
- Disassociate itself from the views of the Church Fathers that demeaned women.
- Teach biblical views of equality of males and females.
- Promote ontological equality, functional equality and vocational equality in policies.
- Change women experiences: Give women equal opportunity around the decision-making tables and positions of leadership. Fill Positions based on ability and not gender
- Replace patriarchal and sexist language with generic, inclusive names and terms.

- Unite to fight against indignities and discrimination of any kind against fellow human beings, regardless of their belief, behaviour, birthplace or gender.
- Protect the unity that Jesus prayed we would have, "That they may be one, even as the Father and I are one". No hierarchy, no inequality, but equality between the sexes.

"For if you remain silent at this time, relief and deliverance for the Jews will arise from another place, but you and your father's family will perish. And who knows but that you have come to your royal position for such a time as this?" Esther 4:14.

Imagine a world where women and children are given the rights stated in the American Declaration of Independence. "That all men are created equal, that they are endowed by their Creator with certain unalienable rights that among these are Life, Liberty, and the pursuit of Happiness."[137]

This book is a call to do just that, for everyone to take responsibility to create a just society that will benefit us all. Of course, this will not happen without illumination as to how we got here. Abuse of women and violence against women can be traced to ill-founded beliefs and perceptions about women.

I trust that you have been enlightened and equipped with many tools to dismantle the edifice of conscious and unconscious bias, male privilege, misogyny, patriarchy and presuppositions, values, and beliefs commonly held about women, often grounded in the misinterpretation of scriptures over millennia. In the words of Prince Harry, "When women are empowered, they immeasurably improve the lives of everyone around them— their families, their communities, and their countries."[138]

---

[137]https://en.wikipedia.org/wiki/United_States_Declaration_of_Independence. (Accessed October 17, 2022).
[138]https://www.independent.co.uk/life-style/women/male-feminist-celebrities-quotes-prince-

I call upon men and women in positions of influence to give women their Value, Visibility, Voice and Vocational opportunities. Society is moving in the direction of a level playing field for all; Churches and other religious communities should step to the front and name the discrimination of women or anyone, in any form, as evil and immoral. **Today the world looks back on slavery as a terrible evil. Tomorrow, the world will look back on our generation and condemn the discrimination of women, just as evil.**

Advocacy for women and girls means happier homes, safer communities, and a relationally healthier society. We celebrate God's gift to man and the final indispensable masterpiece of the universe-Woman. In appreciation for the completeness that women bring to our world and our lives, we bless and salute our women. We "Take a knee" in the cry to end, the pandemic of discrimination, misogyny, abuse, and violence against women and by extension, protect the human family.

I thank you for taking the time to read *Justice for Women: The Cry to End the Pandemic of Discrimination, Intimidation, Misogyny, Abuse, and Violence against Women in Society and Religious Communities*, you are a catalyst to effectuate a seismic change in perspectives and practices on how women are seen and treated in our world. Thank you for joining millions of others in pursuing justice for women and girls.

"I raise my voice—not so I can shout, but so that those without a voice can be heard." – Malala Yousafzai

----

harry-john-legend-a9036986.html (At Climate for Change Concert 2013).

184

Printed in Great Britain
by Amazon